Bible through the
7 Days of Creation

Understanding the times &
knowing what we should do

✝

Stephen Lim

BIBLE THROUGH THE 7 DAYS OF CREATION
Copyright © 2020 by Stephen Lim

All rights reserved. No part of this book may be reproduced or transmitted in any form or by any means without written permission from the author.

ISBN 978-981-14-5263-5

Please visit or contact us at:
- www.issacharb7d.com
- YouTube (search for "Issachar B7D")
- issacharb7d@gmail.com

FREE e-Book available at our website. Paperback and e-Book editions are available at all major online and print distributors worldwide.

Dedication

✝

To my Saviour and Lord Jesus Christ
Who loved and accepted a wretched man like me
Who blessed me with this Gift

&

To my dear wife Wei Ling and daughter Gwyn
Who loved and accepted a wretched man like me
Whom the Giver has blessed me with

Table of Contents

✝

Shalom Aleichem		7
How This Book Came About		9
1.	*Rhema & Kairos*	11
2.	Like the Men of Issachar	13
3.	God's Concept of Time - *Shalom & Shabbat*	15
4.	What the Creation Account Tells Us - *Rhema, Kairos &* Jesus Christ	18
5.	A Thousand Years in a Day	21
6.	Overview of the 7 Days of Creation	23
7.	Day 1: Fall of Man	28
8.	Day 1: Reflections - Who am I? Where are You?	30
9.	Day 2: Flood of Judgment	32
10.	Day 2: Ark of Salvation	34
11.	Day 2: Reflections - Keeping the Faith	36
12.	Day 3: Dry Ground	39
13.	Day 3: Patriarchs	41
14.	Day 3: Exodus	45
15.	First 3 Days of Creation in History	48
16.	Day 4: Greater & Lesser Lights	52

17.	Day 4: Law	55
18.	Day 4: Tabernacle	57
19.	Day 4: Priesthood & Sacrifices	60
20.	Day 4: Reflections - Do This in Remembrance of Me	62
21.	Day 4: Sacred Times	65
22.	Day 4: History of Israel - Part 1 (Israel & Church)	70
23.	Day 4: History of Israel - Part 2 (Lessons from the Wilderness)	74
24.	Day 4: History of Israel - Part 3 (Israel from Yehoshua to Yeshua)	77
25.	Day 4: History of Israel - Part 4 (Church - Commonwealth of Israel)	80
26.	Day 4: Signs of the Times	84
27.	Day 4: Reflections - For Such a Time as This	88
28.	Day 4: Prophets	91
29.	Day 4: Prophetic Narrative & *Rhema* - Part 1 (Understanding the Message)	95
30.	Day 4: Prophetic Narrative & *Rhema* - Part 2 (Discipline vs Judgment)	99
31.	Day 4: Prophetic Narrative & *Rhema* - Part 3 (Day of the Lord & Coming of the *Messiah*)	105
32.	Day 4: Reflections - Gift of Prophecy	109

33.	Day 4: Jesus Christ - Man	111
34.	Day 4: Jesus Christ - Mission	116
35.	Day 4: Jesus Christ - Unwhole Message	120
36.	Day 4: Jesus Christ - Unwelcome Message	123
37.	Day 4: Jesus Christ - Unworldly Message	127
38.	Day 4: Jesus Christ - Un"we" Message	131
39.	Day 5: New Life in the Spirit & Body of Christ	136
40.	Day 5: Acts of the Holy Spirit - From Jerusalem to Babylon	140
41.	Day 5: *Rhema* of the Holy Spirit - Apostolic Message 1 (Faith)	145
42.	Day 5: *Rhema* of the Holy Spirit - Apostolic Message 2 (Hope)	149
43.	Day 5: *Rhema* of the Holy Spirit - Apostolic Message 3 (Love)	153
44.	Day 6: Rule of the Antichrist	159
45.	Day 6: Living in the Last Days	164
46.	Day 6: Tribulation Week	169
47.	Day 7: Day of the Lord	175
48.	Day 7: Millennium	179
49.	At Any Moment? Yes … and No	185
50.	Back to the *Kairos* Now	190

Shalom Aleichem

✝

DEAR Brothers and Sisters in Christ,

Grace and peace to you from our Lord, Saviour and King.

God has an urgent word for His people today so that, like the men of Issachar, we understand the times and know what we should do. What He wants to speak to us is apparent in the Bible when we consider it through the perspective of the 7 Days of Creation - hence the title ***Bible through the 7 Days of Creation*** or B7D in short.

And His word is this - we are fast approaching the end where we will be tested in unprecedented ways. We therefore need to equip ourselves now in our fellowship groups so that we can uphold one another and others in the Body of Christ to keep the faith, persevere in hope, and love the Body, until our Lord returns.

The ***Issachar B7D Fellowship*** is our response in obedience to His word. Through it, God equips us by His people, Word and Spirit. Together with our website and YouTube channel, this book seeks to equip those whom the Lord calls so that they understand the times and know what they should do. The material in this book is based on our YouTube podcasts and is similarly organised into 50 short weekly readings covering the entire Bible in a year, making it conducive for personal or group study and reflection.

As you study God's *Logos* together in your own fellowship groups in whichever local church or denomination you belong to, may His *Rhema* and Spirit transform you into such future and Christ-ready fellowships in His *Kairos*.

For His Glory,
Stephen and Wei Ling Lim
Issachar B7D Fellowship

20 February 2020, Singapore

How This Book Came About
✝

I am a lay believer with my fair share of ups and downs, victories and defeats, in my past 38 years of walking with the Lord since accepting Jesus at the age of 13. Although I have been engaging in some form of personal Bible study or devotion for many years, it was only in 2001 that I started to study the Bible intentionally and systematically. However, I gave up after 7 years and threw away all my writings and materials. I felt empty and exhausted because I had tried to understand God's Word by my own human effort but was going nowhere.

After a long time, God slowly restored me from the ground up. This started with my first fast when He taught me to pray in the Spirit, and then the gift of worship when my playing of the guitar improved tremendously. Then on 6 May 2016, while at a Friday fellowship meeting, an anointed pastor who spoke that evening released a prophetic word to Wei Ling and me. He saw a big clock and all he could think of were the words, *"the time has come."* The time has come for us to move forward out of the wilderness into His plans and purposes for us. Turning to me, he said he saw a scroll and a quill, which meant revelation - that God wanted to speak to me, to tell me things - and that I needed to write them down. I restarted my Bible study and through it, God opened my ears to what He wanted to say to His people through His Word as recorded here.

Although I didn't know then when or where this journey would end, God knew and in His *Kairos* exactly two years later (May 2018) I finished putting down what was needed to be said. It was only a year later that I realized how prophetic God's timing was. God ensured that I finished putting down His word for His people in the year that Israel celebrated 70 years of nationhood since its rebirth in May 1948. It is my personal belief and deep conviction that God's final countdown started from that *Kairos* moment - meaning that some of us will live to witness Christ's return.

May our Lord find us ready when He returns.

1. Rhema & Kairos

†

God has an urgent word for His people today so that, like the men of Issachar, we understand the times and know what we should do. What He wants to speak to us is apparent in the Bible when we consider it through the perspective of the 7 Days of Creation.

THE above summarises what this book is all about. Let us unpack this statement, beginning with:

God has an urgent *word* for His people *today* …

Here, we need to understand the concepts *Rhema* and *Kairos*.

Rhema literally means an "utterance," God speaking to us. This is different from *Logos*, which refers to God's written Word that became flesh in Jesus. So whereas *Logos* is in a sense eternal, *Rhema* is very specific, at a particular point in time. Often, we experience God's *Rhema* when the Holy Spirit prompts or convicts our hearts during our Quiet Times. For instance, we may have read a Bible passage many times before, but one day the words from the passage suddenly "jumps" at us. That is *Rhema*, God speaking to us at that particular moment in time. When God speaks, we are always touched and transformed in some way, because we know that God's word never returns to Him empty (Isaiah 55:11).

Kairos meanwhile refers to that opportune time, usually for some form of action to take place. It is that specially appointed, sacred or set apart time. This is very different from *Chronos* or linear, historical time. Using our example above, when God released His *Rhema* to you, that particular time was His *Kairos* - His opportune, appointed, sacred or set apart time for God to release His word to you. In a sense, we could say that God acted at that moment in time to bring about change in us by simply speaking to us, because we know that God's word has life-transforming power. Often, it also leads us into action as we respond to His *Rhema*.

Before we move on, I want to clarify that we are talking here about God's word - not my word, biblical interpretation or perspective. We are talking about what God wants to say to us and not what we want or choose to hear. Only then is it *Rhema* - God speaking to us and not us trying to decipher the Bible. Also, it is about what God wants to say to us today, to this generation. It is about His *Rhema* for this *Kairos* moment and not for any other generation in history, nor is it about the eternal *Logos* of God. This is the starting point of this book. The question is - do you believe that God really has an urgent word specifically for our generation? I encourage you to prayerfully read on, search the Scriptures for yourself, and ask the Holy Spirit to speak and convict you just as He did with me.

2. Like the Men of Issachar
†

PREVIOUSLY, I spoke about how God had an urgent word for us today, and explained it in terms of *Rhema* and *Kairos*. I then gave the example of how God's *Rhema* and *Kairos* applied in our personal lives.

God has an urgent word for *His people* today ...

However, what we want to focus on here is not about how God speaks to us personally but collectively as His people. In fact, the Bible is primarily God's message to people-groups - Israel, the Church and the nations of this world - and not to individual men and women. God's purpose is so that we, as one Body of Christ, understand the times we live in and know what we together as one people of God should do.

... so that, *like the men of Issachar*, we understand the times and know what we should do.

There is an example of this in the Old Testament. In 1 Chronicles 12:32, when King David was rallying for support from the people to bring Israel under his rule following the death of King Saul, the men of the tribe of Issachar acted decisively to join him because they understood the times - meaning, God's will for the nation then - and knew what Israel should do. Similarly, we believe that God is speaking to His people today and we, like the men of Issachar, need to hear, understand and act decisively as one people of God in light of His *Rhema* and will.

I cannot overemphasise this point, especially in this day and age when we tend to focus only on ourselves and on God's calling for us as individuals. Yes, God may have a unique calling for each one of us, but there is also a general calling for all of us as one Body of Christ. Just like the men of Issachar - I am sure not everyone was called to support David solely as warriors; some would have contributed financially while others helped in unique ways. The point is that they united as a tribe behind the nation of God, brought together by a common understanding and calling that is aligned to God's will for His people at that historic time.

It therefore also means going beyond our home church, which is the local congregation of the Body of Christ, and even looking past our denomination and indeed the worldwide Church itself, to recognise that God's word is for all of His people today. So who are His people? We shall consider this question later. At this point, I just want to emphasise the need to have this universal perspective that goes beyond us as individuals or even beyond our local church or denomination to see who God's people are as God Himself sees it. Let us be like the men of Issachar, who not only saw things from their individual point of view, nor even as a tribe, but as the entire nation of Israel.

3. God's Concept of Time
– *Shalom & Shabbat*

✝

What He wants to speak to us is apparent in the Bible when we consider it through the perspective of the *7 Days of Creation*.

LET us now look at how is it that what God wants to say to His people today - His *Rhema* for us in this *Kairos* - can be discerned from the Bible when we approach it from the viewpoint of the 7 Days of Creation. What is so special about the Creation Account?

To figure this out, we need to understand how God sees Time.

In the spiritual realm, there is no time. What we see happening on earth - whether in the past, present or future - have all reached completion and are finished. There is no beginning and no end - you could say that all is one and done. Moreover, everything is perfect and at rest. Only God can bring about this perfect unity, because it is an expression of His perfect, complete and finished will.

The Hebrew word that describes this perfect finished state is *Shalom*. Now, many of us think that *Shalom* simply means "peace," but it actually means much more. It speaks of completeness or wholeness, health and welfare, safety and soundness, tranquility, prosperity, perfectness, fullness, rest, harmony, the absence of agitation or discord. In short, *Shalom* is the one word that sums up what it means to be in Paradise.

God gave us Time when He created the Heavens and the Earth. Time is always moving forwards and never stops. It is also temporary - we "run out of time" when we die, and Time itself will finally run out when the world ends.

But since we live in time, how are we to visualise what eternity and God's eternal will is like? This spiritual realm where time does not exist and where everything is already complete, perfect and at rest? We are like fish trying to imagine what it is like to live on land.

The answer is that we must view eternity - this "forever and ever" - not like an endless straight line but as a cycle, reflecting the nature of eternity which is more like a circle with no beginning and no end, where everything is one and done in God and at rest.

This is why God gave us the weekly cycle beginning with the 7 Days of Creation. It is no coincidence that the Bible opens with the Creation Week, because it is only when we approach God's *Logos* Word through this cyclical perspective that we will be able to grasp God's eternal will and hear His *Rhema* for us in His *Kairos*. Besides this weekly cycle, God also gave us the monthly and annual cycles, as well as what we call the Sabbatical and Jubilee year cycles.

We will learn more about their significance later but what I want to highlight here is that these cycles all follow a pattern of 7 and is closely connected to the idea of the Sabbath denoting completion, perfection and rest. The Hebrew word for Sabbath - *Shabbat* - comes from the root word *Shin-Beit-Tav*, which means "to cease, to end, to rest," because in the original weekly Sabbath in Genesis 2:1-3, we are told that after God completed or perfected His work of creation on the Sixth Day of Creation, He ceased or ended from His work of creating and rested on the Seventh or Sabbath Day.

Similarly, we have what we call the 7 annual High Sabbaths (connected to 7 Jewish festivals that God commands Israel to celebrate over 7 months every year), the 7th or Sabbatical year, and the 7th by 7th or Jubilee (Sabbatical of Sabbaticals) year.

The Jews greet one another *Shabbat Shalom*, which means "wishing you Sabbath peace," when they meet on the Sabbath. This simple greeting actually carries a very profound message, now that we realise that the 7 Days of Creation, together with these other Sabbatical cycles, are God's way for us to see His eternal will at work on this side of time and history. **God is telling us that, just as in the original Creation Week, there is a future Sabbath or *Shabbat* when this world will enter into His eternal *Shalom*.**

Shabbat Shalom!

4. What the Creation Account Tells Us – *Rhema, Kairos* & Jesus Christ

✝

WE saw how, through the Creation Account, God is telling us that there is a future *Shabbat* when this world will enter into His eternal *Shalom*. But there is even more.

History (*His*-story) is God's story in *action*

First, the Creation Account gives us a framework with which to recognise when God will act in His *Kairos* - His appointed or opportune time. It thus offers us a unique Biblical perspective of world history. History is not just a series of accidents and coincidences or intentional or unintentional human causes and effects. It is His-story, God's story in action, revealing His sovereign will and hand at work over everything that happens in the world. After all, God is the Creator and hence has total mastery over His creation.

The Bible is God's story in *revelation*

But God doesn't just want us to see Him at work. He wants to tell us what to do in light of what He is doing in the world. For this reason, the Creation Account also reveals God's *Rhema* for us in view of the times that we live in. The Bible is God's story in revelation. **Through the Creation Account, each *Kairos***

generation receives a fresh understanding of the Bible and knowledge of what to do according to His eternal will here on earth.

How God's *Rhema* brings about His eternal will in His *Kairos* is seen in the original Creation Week itself. Here, on each appointed day or *Kairos*, God spoke into being - in other words, He acted by releasing His *Rhema* to bring about - an aspect of the unfolding creation according to His eternal will until all is perfect and He rested. Since then, God not only acts by direct divine intervention in the world but also through His people, by releasing His *Rhema* to us in His *Kairos* so that we join together with Him to bring about the outworking of His eternal plan and will until everything is perfect and at rest.

*[God] **made known** [Rhema] to us the mystery of His will according to His good pleasure, which He purposed **in Christ**, to be put into effect **when the times reach their fulfillment** [Kairos] - to bring **unity** [Shalom] to all things in heaven and on earth **under Christ***
- Ephesians 1:9-10

Ultimately though, the Creation Account tells us about Jesus Christ. It reveals how, when God created the world, He had already planned how it would progress and eventually end by bringing all things to perfect completion and rest, forever set apart for Him, in Jesus Christ.

Christ existed from the beginning, came 2,000 years ago to save us, and will return to usher in this Sabbath Day rest (*Shabbat Shalom*). This will happen during His Millennial reign as prophesied in many parts of the Old Testament and especially in Revelations 20.

5. A Thousand Years in a Day

✝

*Teach us to number our days,
that we may gain a heart of wisdom* - Psalm 90:12

EVER since Creation, the people of God can rejoice in the hope of the coming eternal *Shabbat Shalom*. But until then, the Creation Week reveals how history will unfold from the time of Creation until the end of time itself. Here, **each Day of Creation corresponds to each Millennium or a thousand years of world history as determined by the chronology of people and events in the Bible.**

I will be using the rest of this book to demonstrate this, but right now I just want to say that there is a strong biblical basis for this understanding as seen in the following verses:

*With the Lord **a day is like a thousand years**, and a thousand years are like a day* - 2 Peter 3:8

***A thousand years** in Your sight
are like a day that has just gone by,
or like a watch in the night* - Psalm 90:4

Most importantly, this explains Christ's Millennial rule and how the Seventh Day of Creation when God rested in the original Creation Week points to this 1,000-year period when Creation will finally receive its earthly rest.

Creationism or Evolutionism? *Neither!*

At this point, I think it is useful to address the Creationism vs Evolutionism debate.

The real issue here is not whether the world was literally created in 7 days as Creationists believe or had evolved over billions of years according to Evolutionists. All these arguments still function within a narrow viewpoint of the world ruled only by *Chronos*.

Instead, the Creation Account was given to help us understand God's concept of time and eternity, to recognise the signs when He will act in His *Kairos* to bring about His eternal will, and to hear His *Rhema* for His people - in short, to help us understand the times as they relate to God's eternal will and know what we should do. May we, like Moses, ask God to *"teach us to number our days, that we may gain a heart of wisdom."*

6. Overview of the 7 Days of Creation
✝

BEFORE we move on to consider each Day of Creation in detail, let us first have a snapshot of how each of the 7 Days of Creation foreshadows each of the 7 millennia of world history from Creation until now as God unfolds His eternal will both in the world and in His Word.

DAY 1 on the separation of light and darkness foreshadows the **Fall of Man**, resulting in the separation of God (who is synonymous with light) and Man (who was plunged into sin and darkness). This is covered in Genesis 3-4 and is the key event that characterises the First Millennium.

DAY 2 on what the Bible describes as a vault or space separating water from water foreshadows the **Flood** - the first worldwide judgment - and Noah's **Ark** that became that vault separating the rain from the floodwaters. This is covered in Genesis 5-9 and characterises the Second Millennium.

DAY 3 on the gathering of waters and appearing of dry ground foreshadows the emergence of the dry ground of salvation out of the sea of sin and judgment with the call of the **Patriarchs** (Abraham, Isaac and Jacob) and the **Exodus** of the Israelites out of bondage in Egypt - literally through dry ground as they crossed the Red Sea. This is covered in Genesis 10 - Exodus 15 and characterises the Third Millennium.

DAY 4 on the greater and lesser lights foreshadows how God appointed **Israel** - through its Law, Tabernacle, Priesthood, Sacrifices, Sacred Times or Festivals, history and the message of its Prophets - to act as His lesser light pointing mankind to **Jesus Christ**, the Greater and True Light of salvation. This brings us all the way from Exodus 16 to the end of the Gospels and characterises the Fourth Millennium.

DAY 5 on the water and air teeming with life foreshadows the **New Life** available to all through the giving of the Holy Spirit or **Spirit of Christ**, the living waters and very breath of God that gave birth to the Church, the **Body of Christ**. This is covered in the book of Acts and throughout the New Testament Letters and characterises the Fifth Millennium.

DAY 6 on the creation of Adam and the subsequent rule of man foreshadows the coming **Rule of the Antichrist**, the counterfeit "Son of Man." This is covered mainly in Revelations 1-18, but is also spoken of in many other parts of the Bible (especially in the prophetic book of Daniel). The rule of the Antichrist characterises the Sixth Millennium that we are currently living in and defines the spirit of our age.

DAY 7 on the Sabbath rest foreshadows the future **Day of the Lord** when Christ will return to establish His **Millennial Kingdom** here on earth. This is covered in Revelations 19-20 and is also spoken of in many other parts of the Bible. Christ's coming will mark the beginning of the Seventh and final Millennium.

Now, there is an **"Eighth Day" Sabbath** that Jews celebrate after the 7-day Feast of Tabernacles prophetic of Christ's Millennial rule. It foreshadows the final and eternal Sabbath rest as the Heavens, Earth and Time itself will give way to the **New Heaven, Earth and Jerusalem** in eternity. This is covered in the concluding chapters of Revelations 21-22.

The following is a graphical summary (the original slides in this book can be found at www.issacharb7d.com):

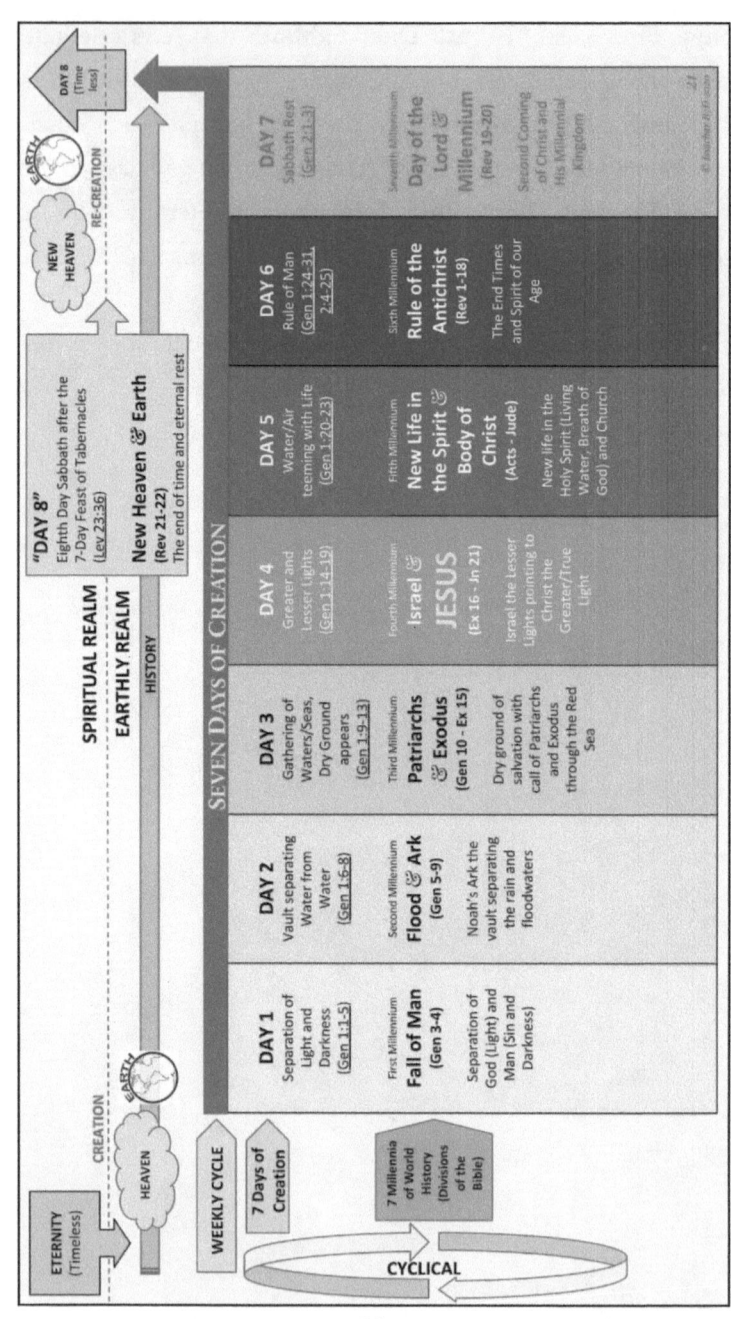

A Note on the Interpretive Approach used in this Book

The interpretive approach used in this book to discern God's *Rhema* as revealed in His Word is similar to the traditional Jewish approach to scriptural interpretation. Here, the **PRDS (Pardes)** approach speaks of 4 progressively deeper levels of interpretation:

Peshat - "plain" (simple) **literal** or direct meaning of the text
Remez - "hints" (deep) **symbolic** or allegorical meaning
Derash - "inquire" (seek) **comparative** meaning or by way of patterns and similar recurrences
Sod - "secret" (mystery) **revelatory** meaning given through divine inspiration of the Holy Spirit

When we apply this approach here, the 7 Days of Creation:

Describes God's original work of Creation **(Literal)**
Points to the 7 millennia of world history **(Symbolic)**
Seeks the meaning/significance of the patterns of 7s seen in the Sabbath, High Sabbath, Sabbatical and Jubilee cycles **(Comparative)**
Ultimately uncovers the mystery regarding the signs of the times and Jesus' soon return in our generation **(Revelatory)**

7. Day 1: Fall of Man

✝

*In the beginning God created the heavens and the earth. Now the earth was **formless** and **empty**, **darkness** was over the surface of the deep, and the Spirit of God was hovering over the waters.*

*And God said, **"Let there be light,"** and there was light. God saw that the **light was good**, and He **separated the light from the darkness**. God called the light "day," and the darkness He called "night." And there was evening, and there was morning - the first day*
- Genesis 1:1-5

THE First Day of Creation tells us that God created light.

In fact, Jesus is the True Light.

Light is associated with good and cannot co-exist with darkness, which is synonymous with evil. God is not the author of evil. The Apostle John tells us that *"God is light; in Him there is no darkness at all"* (1 John 1:5). Evil exists as a result of free choice. Evil is the absence of good or light, when we choose darkness.

The First Day also tells us about the Fall of Man. Because of sin, our starting point - like that of Creation - is darkness. The Apostle Paul tells us that *"all have sinned and fall short of the glory* (light) *of God"* (Romans 3:23). Separated from God as darkness is from light, we are left formless and empty. In the dark, we cannot see ourselves or our surroundings. We do not know who or where we are, what we ought to become or where we ought to be headed. Instead, just as darkness flees from the light, our tendency whenever we sin is to run away or hide our shame and wrongdoing from God just like what Adam and Eve did (Genesis 3:8). Like Cain, we are condemned to become *"restless wanderers"* (Genesis 4:12) here on earth. Now, the most wonderful part is that God already knew all this from the very beginning. And only He can reconcile us back to Him in Jesus.

8. Day 1: Reflections - Who am I? Where are You?

✝

AS we end this very brief section on the First Day of Creation, let us reflect on the 2 questions above:

*But you are a chosen people, a royal priesthood, a holy nation, God's special possession, that you may declare the praises of Him **who called you out of darkness into His wonderful light*** - 1 Peter 2:9

*For God, who said, "Let light shine out of darkness," **made His light shine in our hearts** to give us the light of the knowledge of God's glory displayed in the face of Christ* - 2 Corinthians 4:6

First, Who am I? Because of the Fall of Adam, we are born into sin and darkness, doomed to a life that is separated from God and that will eventually end in physical and eternal or spiritual death. We are formless and empty, just as how Creation was at the very beginning. Here, it is interesting that the Jews start their day at sunset, unlike most of us whose day begins at sunrise. We could almost say that it is God's way of reminding them daily about how we start in sin and darkness, just as our day begins at sunset. However, not all is gloom and doom. The good news is that although we may have started in sin and darkness, it doesn't mean that this defines our end point and true identity. The verses above tell us that in Christ,

God has called us out of darkness into His wonderful light, the same way He called light out of darkness. He, who made light shine out of darkness, made His light shine into our hearts through knowing Christ. And just as He declares light to be good, God declares us good - because we are His children and bear His image, the same way we resemble our earthly parents.

But the LORD God called to the man "Where are you?" - Genesis 3:9

Next, Where are you? Do we find ourselves in a pit or a place where we feel there is no return? If we do, whose voice do we hear? Is it the voice of accusation, shame, guilt and despair? That it is too late and that God will never take us back? Or do we hear His voice of truth, tenderly calling us, seeking us as a shepherd looks for his one lost sheep, a father his lost son? Would God ask where we are if He is not looking for us? Or are we in our comfort zone, thinking that all is well? We may think that we are in a safe place, since our sins are "lesser" than many others around us. God knows where we are, but do we know ourselves? Are we where we ought to be, in the Father's House and in His Son's embrace? Like the prodigal younger son in Jesus' parable of the 2 sons, we need to come to the realization and acceptance of where we are (and are not) before we can repent and turn back to where we ought to be - with God. And God will receive us "Just as I am," wherever we may be coming back from. Otherwise, we will always remain restless wanderers.

9. Day 2: Flood of Judgment
✝

*And God said, "Let there be a vault between the **waters** to separate **water** from **water**." So God made the vault and separated the **water** under the vault from the **water** above it. And it was so. God called the vault "sky." And there was evening, and there was morning - the second day* - Genesis 1:6-8

IF the First Day of Creation speaks of us how we are in darkness, being separated from the light of the glory of God because of our sin, then the Second Day reveals how, as a result, we stand under judgment by a holy and righteous God. Sin demands a price, which must be paid, and this price is death (Romans 6:23).

We see this fulfilled in the Great Flood, the first worldwide judgment.

In order to better understand how this event could happen, remember how the world was formless, empty and dark in the beginning, and the Spirit of God was hovering over the waters. The Bible tells us that the world was initially covered in water, for it was only on the Second Day that part of this water was separated out and lifted up into the atmosphere, and on the Third Day that dry ground first appeared when the remaining waters were gathered in the deepest parts of the earth. The Flood came about when God released all these waters stored above the sky and beneath the earth back onto the world. For those of you who doubt whether this global catastrophe actually took place, there are over 270 accounts of it from people groups and cultures all over the world.

As we conclude, I just want to make 2 observations:

First, 1656 years passed from the time of Adam until the Flood. During this time, only 8 (Noah's family) survived out of possibly 3-7 billion people that lived then. Noah's father Lamech was 56 when Adam died at age 930, meaning that most of mankind would have heard first-hand from Adam about God, yet they still turned to evil. Imagine how heart-wrenching it was for Adam but even more so for God!

> *And I will put enmity*
> *between you and the woman,*
> *and between your offspring and hers;*
> *He will crush your head,*
> *and you will strike His heel"* - Genesis 3:15

Second, following the Fall, God promised Adam and Eve an offspring who would crush Satan's head and so redeem mankind. They must have harboured this hope when Cain - literally the first "son of man" - was born. But instead of crushing Satan, Cain murdered his own brother, Abel. We are just so utterly sinful, unable to rescue ourselves. Only God Himself - when He came to us as Jesus the True Son of Man - is able to crush Satan and cover the nakedness and shame of our sins.

10. Day 2: Ark of Salvation

✝

*And God said, "Let there be a **vault** between the waters to separate water from water"* - Genesis 1:6

LOOKING back, we see that God had been merciful indeed. He did not destroy mankind immediately but waited patiently for over 1,600 years, holding back His judgment so that they could repent and return to Him.

And God did not just sit back and do nothing during this period.

He warned them through Enoch of the coming judgment. Enoch, who was interestingly the seventh generation from Adam, prophesied:

"See, the Lord is coming with thousands upon thousands of His holy ones to judge everyone, and to convict all of them of all the ungodly acts they have committed in their ungodliness, and of all the defiant words ungodly sinners have spoken against Him" - Jude 1:14-15

Enoch even named his son Methuselah (meaning "his death shall bring") as God's message to the wicked, for when Methuselah died, his death brought about the Great Flood that same year (Genesis 5:25-29, 7:6).

And God did not just wait and warn. The Second Day of Creation ultimately reveals how God actively worked out His plan of salvation for mankind through Noah's Ark - this "vault" as it were separating the flood water below it from the rain water above during the first judgment.

This first ark ultimately points to Jesus, our Spiritual Ark of salvation. In 1 Peter 3:20-22, the Apostle Peter explains how just as Noah and his family were saved through water by the ark, rising above God's flood judgment, we are now saved through the water of baptism as we put our faith in Jesus, who by His resurrection lifts us up from death to life and from God's coming judgment of fire at the end of time.

Indeed, Noah is a picture of Christ. His name means "comfort/rest," pointing to Christ our ultimate Giver of comfort (John 14:18) and *Shalom* rest (Matthew 11:28). And not only Noah. God actually reveals His wonderful plan of salvation in Jesus through the meaning of the names of the ten generations from Adam to Noah!

Man (**Adam**) appointed (**Seth**) mortal (**Enosh**) sorrow (**Kenan**).

The Blessed God (**Mahalalel**) shall come down (**Jared**) teaching (**Enoch**).

His death shall bring (**Methuselah**) the despairing (**Lamech**) comfort/rest (**Noah**).

11. Day 2: Reflections – Keeping the Faith
✝

As it was in the days of Noah, so it will be at the coming of the Son of Man - Matthew 24:37

AS we end this section on the Second Day of Creation, I want to draw your attention to the prophetic significance of this period of time for us today.

In Matthew 24:37-39, Jesus tells us that when He comes back, the world will be like that during the days of Noah. For in those days before the Great Flood, people were eating and drinking, marrying and giving in marriage, up to the day Noah entered the ark. They knew nothing about what would happen until the flood waters swept them all away. We saw how the Flood only came after 1656 years, which is a very long time indeed. Enoch was born 622 years after Creation, meaning mankind would have heard Enoch's warning of God's coming judgment for over a millennium. But since nothing happened to the world for such a long time, they doubted and ignored his warnings. By Noah's time, no one was listening.

Today, we are living in such a world that Jesus warns us about. It has been almost 2,000 years since He first came to save us. The Bible warns us that Jesus will soon return in judgment but since nothing has happened for such a long time, we doubt and ignore God's Word. However, as we will see in this book, the days of Noah are indeed here.

The question therefore is, do we recognise the times that we live in now? Is our ark - our faith in Christ - secure?

Are we like the wise or foolish builders Jesus speaks about in Matthew 7:24-27, able to withstand the rains, storms and floods of trouble and persecution that will strike before He returns?

Have we put on the full armour of God so that when the day of evil comes, we may be able to stand our ground, and after we have done everything, to stand (Ephesians 6:10-17)?

Are we able to finally declare as Paul did, *"I have fought the good fight, I have finished the race, I have kept the faith"* (2 Timothy 4:7)?

As we reflect on these questions, we need to:

Change our perspective if we are to understand the times we live in and know what we should do. We need to listen to God's *Rhema* in this *Kairos* and not remain in ignorance or unbelief.

Know who and where we are in Christ, to turn on and be guided by our spiritual GPS to discover and follow God's eternal purposes for us and not run after the futile ways of this world.

Live holy and separated lives - We can expect the end times to be like the days of Noah. Life will seem normal with people eating and drinking, marrying and giving in marriage, not knowing what will happen until the end suddenly strikes. Consequently, we need to build not our worldly livelihood but our ark of faith in Christ so that we will keep the faith when the rains, storms and floods come.

12. Day 3: Dry Ground
✝

*And God said, "Let the water under the sky be gathered to one place, and **let dry ground appear**." And it was so. God called the dry ground "land," and the gathered waters He called "seas." And God saw that it was good.*

Then God said, "Let the land produce vegetation … And God saw that it was good. And there was evening, and there was morning - the third day
- Genesis 1:9-13

THE Third Day of Creation concerns the emergence of dry ground and the life that came along with it. It points to how, following the Great Flood, God literally gathered the waters so that life could once again be revived on the dry ground of a new world.

Babylon *vs* Jerusalem

But mankind continued to drown in the sea of sin and judgment due to their fallen nature. Beginning with the Tower of Babel, Man created a kingdom for himself to oppose God. This kingdom of man is represented by the ancient city of Babylon that emerged from the ruins of Babel. It is hostile to the Kingdom of God, which is represented by the Holy City of Jerusalem, and will eventually be used by Satan in his final confrontation with God in the end times.

Abraham Israel Jesus

*The LORD had said to **Abram** …*
*"I will make you into a great **nation**,*
and I will bless you;
I will make your name great,
and you will be a blessing.
I will bless those who bless you,
and whoever curses you I will curse;
*and **all peoples on earth***
will be blessed through you"
- Genesis 12:1-3

So, symbolically, God brought forth "dry ground" as it were, which is His plan to rescue us. God chose one man, Abraham, and from Abraham and his descendants, God birthed a nation, Israel, and it is through Israel that all peoples on earth are blessed, because out of this nation God gave us Jesus.

13. Day 3: Patriarchs
✝

WHEN we look at how God brought about this dry ground of salvation through the lives of the Patriarchs Abraham, Isaac and Jacob, we learn some very important lessons about our Christian faith.

*Abram **believed** the LORD, and He credited it to him as **righteousness*** - Genesis 15:6

First, God's gift of eternal life is unconditional, meaning we cannot do anything to earn our salvation. It only requires faith on our part. Like Abraham, we are to believe in God alone and in His word for us in order for God to credit or give us His righteousness to cover our sinfulness.

In Ephesians 2:8-9, Paul says, *"For it is by grace you have been saved, through faith - and this is not from yourselves, it is the gift of God - not by works, so that no one can boast."* Hebrews 11:6 tells us that, *"without faith it is impossible to please God."*

*Now you, brothers and sisters, like Isaac, are **children of promise*** - Galatians 4:28

What this means also is that, as Christians, we are children of promise like Isaac. Just as God promised Abraham a son and the blessing of descendants as numerous as the stars in the sky,

God promises us His very own Son Jesus and the blessing of becoming Abraham's spiritual descendants and the very children of God.

Paul in Romans 9:7-8 tells us that *"not all of Abraham's human children are really God's children. Instead, it is only those children who were born as a result of God's promise. Only they are the people that God calls Abraham's children."* We do not become Christians by being born into Christian families. Neither do we become Christians by trying to earn God's favour through our religious or good works. We become God's children of promise only through faith in Christ, when we enter into a personal saving relationship with Him.

In *His* time (God's *Kairos*)

In view of this, we need to wait on God and not run ahead of Him. This is the main lesson behind Jacob's life. Although he was already assured of God's promises (Genesis 25:23, Romans 9:10-13), Jacob did not wait for God's *Kairos* but rushed ahead to try to steal the blessing. This led to a life on the run filled with lies and deception.

Instead, we are to be like Joseph, who understood God's *Kairos* and therefore knew what he should do. Let me elaborate. Time is God's gift to us. Our time thus belongs to God, and the best time for us is always His *Kairos*. In His wisdom and love, God gave His creation 7 Days or 7,000 years to make everything perfect, complete and at rest (*Shalom*). When Adam and Eve sinned, God in His mercy sent them out of Eden away from the Tree of Life so that they would not eat from this tree and end up spending eternity in darkness, doom and death. In His time, God gave us a second chance through one man, Noah, and called another, Abraham, through whom we could be saved, promising him a son.

But Abraham could not wait; he rushed ahead in his own time. Yet God is faithful. In His time, He fulfilled His promise to give Abraham a son, Isaac. In His time, Isaac had twins, and God chose the younger, Jacob. But Jacob could not wait; he rushed ahead in his own time. Yet God is faithful. In His time, He wrestled Jacob into submission and through his dysfunctional family of 12 sons, brought forth the nation Israel. In His time, He revealed His plans to Jacob's favourite son, Joseph, in a dream, which led to the beginning of his living nightmare. Joseph was sold as a slave into Egypt and later imprisoned on false charges.

You intended to harm me, but God intended it for good to accomplish what is now being done, the saving of many lives - Genesis 50:20

But Joseph knew God and trusted in His faithfulness. He did not rush ahead in his own time but waited on God's time. So, in God's time, Joseph was appointed to the highest position in Egypt after Pharaoh. In His time, God brought to pass His plans as revealed in Joseph's dreams, and brought Joseph face-to-face with his wicked brothers. But Joseph did not harbour anger and bitterness towards them. He knew God and recognised His time and purpose; it was God who sent him ahead into Egypt to preserve a remnant by a great deliverance. In His time, God used one man, Joseph - who understood the signs of the times and knew what he had to do - as part of His larger salvation plan for us all.

Today, do we acknowledge that our time belongs to God? Do we know Him well enough and trust in His faithfulness to wait on His *Kairos* and not rush ahead in our own time? Do we know His heart and His purpose so that we can recognise the signs of the times that we live in today and know what we ought to do in such a time as this?

14. Day 3: Exodus
†

THERE was one more *Kairos* event that took place on the Third Day of Creation - the supernatural gathering of the waters and appearing of dry ground during the Exodus of the Israelites from slavery in Egypt.

Now, most of us are quite familiar with this event and how it is a picture of our deliverance from bondage to sin when we accept Jesus as our personal Saviour and Lord. But there is another, perhaps even more important point that I wish to highlight. For it is here that God first revealed His personal name.

> *Then say to Pharaoh, 'This is what the LORD says: Israel is **My firstborn son*** - Exodus 4:22

Let me explain. Although God's name *Yahweh* (usually translated as LORD) is first mentioned in Genesis 2:4, this is because Genesis was written by Moses, whom God revealed His name to. So while we read of the children of Seth, as well as Abraham and Isaac *"calling on the name of the LORD"* (Genesis 4:26, 12:8, 13:4, 21:33, 26:25), we are told in Exodus 6:2-3 that God did not reveal His personal name to them, not even when asked by Jacob after wrestling the whole night with God (Genesis 32:29-30). It was only here with Moses that God revealed His personal name, and we are told the reason - *"Israel is My firstborn son."* God saved the Israelites because He loved them as His very own. He saved His people not just to free them from their physical bondage but to restore their true identity as His children.

REFLECTIONS - My Father's Name

*"Not everyone who says to Me, 'Lord, Lord,' will enter the kingdom of heaven, but only the one who does the will of My Father who is in heaven. Many will say to Me on that day, 'Lord, Lord, did we not prophesy **in Your name** and **in Your name** drive out demons and **in Your name** perform many miracles?' Then I will tell them plainly, **I never knew you**. Away from Me, you evildoers!'* - Matthew 7:21-23

Unfortunately, many seek God's name for the wrong reasons, often for power or control, blessings or self-glory. Yes, we are told of the power found in His name alone, that *"Everyone who calls on the name of the LORD will be saved"* (Joel 2:32, Acts 2:21, Romans 10:13). The verses above tell us that we can prophesy, drive out demons and perform many miracles in His name. However, when God proclaimed His name to the Israelites, it was because they were to be His children, His firstborn, who would carry His name to all the world. Likewise, when Jesus took on the name of God - "I AM" (John 6:35, 8:12, 10:9, 10:11, 11:25, 14:6, 15:1; see also John 8:58) - it was not to seek glory for Himself although He could have easily done so, but to do His Father's will. God gave us His name in Jesus to let us know that He is our Father and we are His children.

It is this personal relationship that is the key to true discipleship. When we see God as our Heavenly Father, we are motivated by love and obedience, and His will and honour becomes what is most important in our lives. It was this love, love for His Father and love for us His brothers and sisters, that led Jesus to obey and do His Father's will by dying on the Cross for us.

Ultimately, it is God Himself who demonstrates true love to us His children. In Jesus' parable of the prodigal son, the father is the true prodigal by his extravagant, even reckless and wasteful show of love to his prodigal son. But this was exactly what God did for us as Paul explains in Romans 5:8. Like the father who rushes out of his home to meet his unworthy son, *"God demonstrates his own love for us in this: While we were still sinners,* [God left His heavenly home and came down to us in the form of a man in] *Christ* [and] *died for us."*

15. First 3 Days of Creation in History

✝

AT this point, I want to show how the first 3 Days of Creation fit into our Biblical perspective of world history, where each day corresponds to a millennium of world history as determined by the chronology of people and events in the Bible.

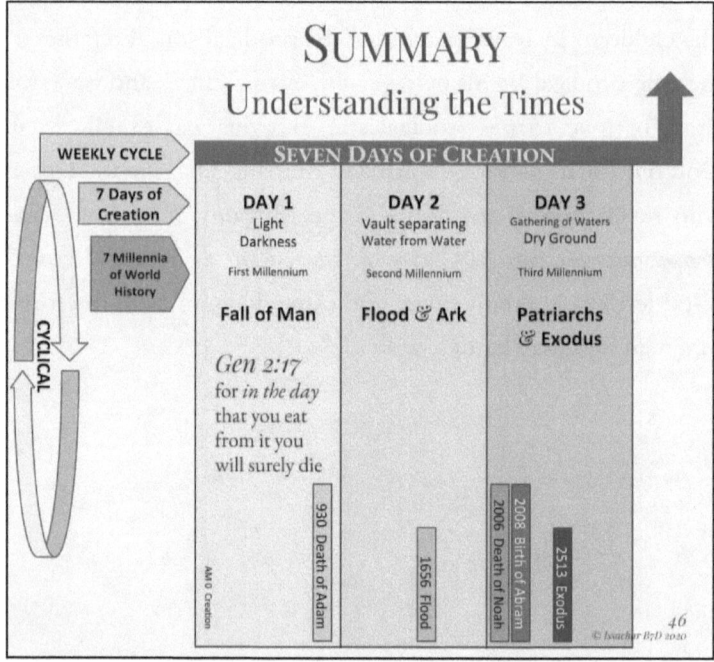

Note: Dates are based on AM (*Anno Mundi*) which is the year after the creation of the world.

First, we saw how **DAY 1** foreshadowed sin and its consequences in the **Fall of Man**. In Genesis 2:17, God warned Adam not to eat from the tree of the knowledge of good and evil, for in the day he ate from it he would surely die. If a day is indeed like a thousand years, then Adam truly died within the day at age 930. In fact, none lived beyond a thousand years.

Then we saw how **DAY 2** foreshadowed impending judgment and salvation through the **Flood** and **Noah's Ark**. The Flood happened in the Second Millennium in AM 1656. Noah lived another 350 years after the Flood and died in AM 2006, marking the end of Day 2.

Finally, we saw how **DAY 3** foreshadowed God's dry ground of salvation with the **Patriarchs** and **Exodus**. Abraham was born at the start of the Third Millennium in AM 2008, 2 years after Noah died. The Exodus also took place on Day 3 in AM 2513.

We also see glimpses of Jesus throughout this period:

Melchizedek - This mysterious king, who ruled over Jerusalem and whom Abraham gave a tenth of his possessions, is also said to be a *"priest of God Most High."* The Bible later describes Jesus as both King and Priest from the line of Melchizedek.

12 tribes of Israel - Their names point to Jesus just like the ten generations from Adam to Noah.

> Behold a son (**Reuben**) is born to us, for God heard (**Simeon**) us and became attached to (**Levi**) us.
>
> Praise the Lord (**Judah**)! He has vindicated (**Dan**) my struggle (**Naphtali**) and brought good fortune (**Gad**), happiness (**Asher**), reward (**Issachar**) and honour (**Zebulun**).
>
> He added (**Joseph**) to us a son of righteousness (**Benjamin**).

***Messiah* ben Joseph, the Lamb of God** - In Joseph, Jesus the *Messiah* (meaning the "Anointed One") is revealed, firstly, as a man of suffering and sorrow. He is the True Passover Lamb of God who died so that God's judgment will pass over our sins. And through Joseph's son Ephraim (see explanation below), the way of salvation is open to all nations. Jesus fulfilled all these in His first coming as Saviour of the world.

***Messiah* ben Judah, the Lion of Judah** - In Judah, Jesus the *Messiah* is ultimately revealed as the conquering King of Kings, the Lion of Judah who will rule all nations. This will come to pass when Jesus returns as the Lord of Lords to usher in His Millennial Kingdom.

Ephraim and the Fullness of the Gentiles - When Jacob died, God's blessings that were inherited by him were passed on to his 12 sons. Joseph received a double portion usually given to the firstborn when Jacob took Joseph's sons, Manasseh and Ephraim, as his own. In blessing the younger son Ephraim, Jacob further prophesied that Ephraim's descendants *"will become a **multitude*** [fullness] ***of*** [Gentile or non-Jewish] ***nations***" (Genesis 48). In so doing, Jacob was reaffirming God's promise to his grandfather that all the peoples on earth would be blessed through Abraham and Israel.

*Israel has experienced a hardening in part until the **full number of the Gentiles** has come in, and in this way all Israel will be saved*
- Romans 11:25-26

This prophecy came to pass during Jesus' first coming in a most unexpected way. By rejecting and crucifying Jesus, Israel actually became part of God's plan to save the world. In fact, Israel's continued hardening towards God contributed to the Gospel being brought to the Gentile world, most notably by Paul. In Romans 11:11-32, Paul drew this connection but also prophesied of a future day when Israel would return to God, once *"the full number of the Gentiles has come in."* We will explore this very important point in detail later on.

16. Day 4: Greater & Lesser Lights
†

*And God said, "Let there be lights in the vault of the sky to **separate** the day from the night, and let them serve as signs to **mark** sacred times, and days and years, and let them be lights in the vault of the sky to **give light** on the earth." And it was so. God made two great lights - the **greater light** to govern the day and the **lesser light** to govern the night. He also made the stars. God set them in the vault of the sky to give light on the earth, to govern the day and the night, and to separate light from darkness. And God saw that it was good. And there was evening, and there was morning - the fourth day* - Genesis 1:14-19

THE Fourth Day of Creation concerns the creation of specific lights.

First, to separate day from night. Symbolically, this speaks of the separation of good from bad, holy from unholy.

Second, to serve as signs to mark sacred times, and days and years. We learnt previously that the sacred times are God's opportune times or *Kairos* when He will act in the *Chronos* of world history to bring about His will. The lights are meant to guide, indicate and draw our attention to these *Kairos* events even as the days and years roll by.

Third, to give light on the earth. Symbolically, to illuminate or make clear to mankind not just what is good or holy or sacred, but ultimately to reveal God Himself to us.

God made 2 great lights - the greater light to govern the day and the lesser light to govern the night. In the original Creation Account, the greater light refers to the rising sun that marks the end of night and dawn of a new day, while the lesser light refers to the moon.

Because of the tender mercy of our God,
by which the rising sun will come to us from heaven - Luke 1:78

Prophetically, the greater light refers to Jesus the risen Son of God who marks the end of the darkness and night of sin and death and the dawn of a new day in the light, righteousness and life of God.

"I will also make you a light for the Gentiles,
that My salvation may reach to the ends of the earth" - Isaiah 49:6b

The lesser light meanwhile refers to God's chosen people and nation, Israel. It is not coincidental that the first thing Israel did as a nation was to sanctify or set apart the new moon (Exodus 12:1-2). Instead of using the sun (solar calendar) to measure time, Israel was to use the moon (lunar calendar). Instead of starting the day at sunrise, they were to start the day at sundown (or you could call it moonrise).

"You are the light of the world" - Matthew 5:14a

The lesser light also refers to the Church.

Now, there is a reason God used the sun to refer to Jesus and the moon to refer to His people. For just as the moon does not have light in itself but reflects the light of the sun, both Israel and the Church are called by God to reflect His glory as ultimately revealed in Jesus so as to draw all nations to Him.

17. Day 4: Law
✝

WE will now examine how Israel fulfilled God's plan to be His lesser light leading us to Jesus. Buckle up as we cover 864 chapters or 72.7% of the entire Bible in the next 16 readings!

Let us begin by looking at how God first equipped Israel for this purpose.

*"'You will be for Me a **kingdom of priests** and a **holy nation**.' These are the words you are to speak to the Israelites"* - Exodus 19:6

When God rescued the Israelites from slavery in Egypt, His reason was not only to preserve His chosen people out of whom Jesus would come. They were also to become His Kingdom of priests and holy nation to draw all nations to worship the One True God in Jesus.

God prepared Israel for this role during its one-year stopover at Mount Sinai following its escape from Egypt by first giving the nation His Law - also known as the Law of Moses or more commonly as the Ten Commandments. The Law is like a National Constitution or Agreement binding Israel to God. In Exodus 19:5, God told Israel, *"Now if you obey Me fully and keep My covenant, then out of all nations you will be My treasured possession."*

The Bible tells us that Israel failed to keep God's Law. In fact, none of us is able to meet up to God's standard of righteousness. In Romans 3:20, Paul tells us, *"Therefore no one will be declared righteous in God's sight by the works of the law; rather, through the law we become conscious of our sin."*

*Do not think that I have come to abolish the Law or the Prophets; I have not come to abolish them but to **fulfill** them* - Matthew 5:17

No one, that is, except Jesus. When God gave Israel the Law, the Israelites thought that the Law was given for them to follow in perfect obedience. They did not understand God's real intention, which was actually for Israel - by their very failure to keep the Law - to thereby lift up the Law like a banner before the entire world to expose our utter sinfulness and inability to meet God's standard of righteousness and holiness, and therefore our great need for Jesus, who alone is able to fulfill the requirements of the Law (Galatians 3:24, Romans 3:19-24, 4:15, 7:7, 8:3-4, 10:4). God already knew that neither Israel nor any of us for that matter would be able to perfectly obey the Law. His purpose in giving Israel the Law was so that through it, Israel would unwittingly serve as God's lesser light uncovering man's true condition and pointing them to the only One who could save them.

18. Day 4: Tabernacle

✝

*Then have them make a **sanctuary** for Me, and I will **dwell** among them* - Exodus 25:8

BECAUSE Israel was never meant to be able to uphold the Law, God also provided the nation with the Tabernacle, a special place or sanctuary whereby they and all mankind could come before God, as well as a system of Priesthood and Sacrifices. These were to provide a way for Israel to be forgiven and cleansed so that it could serve as God's priest drawing all nations to worship the One True God. Israel was to be God's lesser light not by its own righteousness but by reflecting God's love, grace, mercy and forgiveness to the world.

Now, if the Law is meant to expose our sinfulness and inability to come into God's presence by our good works, then the Tabernacle reveals how God nonetheless wants to dwell among us by providing a way to remove this barrier of sin. If the Law tells us how we are to *"love the Lord your God with all your heart and with all your soul and with all your mind ...* [and to] *love your neighbor as yourself"* (Matthew 22:37-40), then the Tabernacle speaks of how it is God who first loves us. For God, love is not just mere words or something demanded of us by command. Instead, He makes the first move to restore our broken relationship with Him.

Ultimately, the Tabernacle points to Jesus - *Immanuel* or "God with us" (Matthew 1:23).

We are told that this earthly Tabernacle is patterned after the *"true tabernacle"* in heaven (Hebrews 8:1-5, 9:11, 24). Besides its earthly function, it is meant to reflect a deeper spiritual reality, which can be summed up by Jesus in John 14:6 - *"I am the Way and the Truth and the Life. No one comes to the Father except through Me."*

Jesus is the only Way to God - We see this reflected in the single entrance into the Tabernacle. And not only that. In order for the priests to enter the covered tent proper, they have to offer burnt sacrifices on the altar and wash themselves at the bronze basin. These are symbolic of how we cannot enter into God's presence unless we accept Jesus' bodily sacrifice on the cross for us and let our sins be cleansed and washed away by His blood.

Jesus is the Truth that reveals God to us - Once inside what is known as the Holy Place, the only source of light in the tent comes from the golden lampstand - symbolic of Jesus, our True Light. Jesus is also reflected in the Table of Showbread, also known as the bread of the presence or that which causes God to "show up." In Jesus, God literally "showed up" among us. He is God's Word made flesh, the Bread of Life, the Truth that sets us free.

Jesus is Life itself - Hebrews 10:19-20 tells us that *"we have confidence to enter the Most Holy Place (where the Ark of the Covenant and the Glory of God resided) ... by a new and living way opened for us through the curtain (or veil), that is, His body."* For when Jesus died, we are told that the curtain in the Temple that separated us from the life-giving presence of God in the Most Holy Place was torn in two. In Jesus, we can now boldly come before God to receive eternal life.

19. Day 4: Priesthood & Sacrifices
✝

I mentioned earlier that God instituted a system of Priesthood and Sacrifices in order for Israel to serve as His Kingdom of priests drawing all nations to worship Him at the Tabernacle. But these institutions were all imperfect and insufficient.

God chose Moses' elder brother Aaron to be the High Priest and their tribe - the Levites - as priests. But they, like the rest of the Israelites and indeed mankind, were sinful and fallen individuals.

The blood of the animal sacrifices were also only of symbolic value and could not really atone or serve as payment for man's sin. The author of Hebrews tells us how, *"Day after day every priest stands and performs his religious duties; again and again he offers the same sacrifices, which can never take away sins ...* [because] *it is impossible for the blood of bulls and goats to take away sins"* (Hebrews 10:11, 4). Surely we do not think that an animal could take our place. We are made in the image of God and therefore only one among us but who is perfect in God's eyes could properly pay the price for our sins.

> *But when this Priest* [Jesus] *had offered **for all time** one sacrifice for sins, He sat down at the right hand of God* - Hebrews 10:12

God's ultimate intention is for Aaron and the Levitical priesthood to point to Jesus, our true and perfect Great High Priest, whom we saw before is of the mysterious priestly and royal line of Melchizedek. Meanwhile, the inadequate animal sacrifices that have to be offered day after day, year after year, point to the all-sufficient sacrifice of Jesus the Lamb of God, the only perfect and sinless man who can therefore by His one sacrifice atone for the sins of mankind for all time.

20. Day 4: Reflections - Do This in Remembrance of Me

✝

*For I received from the Lord what I also passed on to you: The Lord Jesus, on the night He was betrayed, took bread, and when He had given thanks, He broke it and said, "This is My body, which is for you; **do this in remembrance of Me**." In the same way, after supper He took the cup, saying, "This cup is the new covenant in My blood; **do this, whenever you drink it, in remembrance of Me**." For whenever you eat this bread and drink this cup, you **proclaim the Lord's death until He comes*** - 1 Corinthians 11:23-26

WHY do we celebrate Holy Communion?

For most of us, it is to remember and proclaim the Lord's death (1 Corinthians 11:26a). Here, the bread and wine signify His body and blood given to save us.

Jesus our *Passover Lamb*

Jesus gave us this command during His Last Supper with His disciples. This meal took place on the eve of the annual Jewish festival of the Passover, which is to commemorate how God's judgment passed over the Israelites the night before their exodus from slavery in Egypt 1,500 years earlier. As part of the Passover celebration, Jews are to sacrifice and eat the Passover lamb like how their ancestors did.

This lamb ultimately points to Jesus, our True Passover Lamb who was sacrificed one appointed (*Kairos*) Passover Day 2,000 years ago so that God's eternal judgment will pass over us. He is the perfect Lamb of God who died for our sins. Jesus is also the True Bread that came down from heaven to give us eternal life, like the Manna that God sent to sustain the Israelites during their wilderness journey to the Promised Land. In Jesus' death, God revealed His love for us, adopting us as His children at the price of His only Son.

Jesus our *Bridegroom* at the *Wedding Feast of the Lamb*

However, Jesus' death is also the dowry and bride price to make us His bride again. The bread symbolises Jesus' body offered anew to us in marriage that we may become one flesh with Him in resurrection, giving new meaning to His words, *"you are in Me, and I am in you"* (John 14:20). The cup of wine meanwhile symbolises Jesus' blood of the New Covenant, which is essentially a new marriage contract.

When Israel failed to keep the Law - her old marriage contract with God - the punishment was supposed to be divorce or death (Leviticus 20:10, Deuteronomy 24:1-4). But God in His great love and mercy did neither. He chose instead to die in our place to pay the price for our spiritual adultery. He then rewrote the marriage contract, this time not on tablets of stone but on our hearts, paying the bride price again with His own blood and sealing it with the Holy Spirit so as to guarantee our eternal union with Him.

We could say that Jesus performed 2 miracles at 2 weddings, one at the start and the other at the end of His ministry - turning water into wine in Cana (His first miracle), and turning wine into blood (His final miracle, spiritually speaking). In these acts, we see why He is our living water that wells up to eternal life.

The Bible speaks of at least 2 weddings and a funeral as we see here, but of only one marriage made in Heaven - that of the Lamb and His Bride. Until that Day, until He comes (1 Corinthians 11:26b), we are called to celebrate the Holy Communion, to share in common the bread and wine representing Jesus' body and blood. When we do so, let us remember that **it is not so much about the gift as it is about the Giver.** It is not so much about us and the joy of our salvation, our exodus from bondage to sin and journey to the eternal Promised Land. It is about our great God and His sacrificial love to restore our broken relationship with Him as His children and Jesus' redeemed bride. In this way, we truly honour God by *"do*[ing] *this in remembrance of Me* [Jesus].*"

21. Day 4: Sacred Times
✝

PREVIOUSLY, we learnt about God's concept of Time and how He gave us a series of Sabbatical cycles as a way for us, who live in earthly time, to understand His eternal will.

These were given in the form of religious practices and festivals, as well as national laws and regulations, that Israel is to observe on specific days every week (Sabbath), year (High Sabbath), Sabbatical year, and Jubilee year to mark sacred times.

God's purpose was for Israel to draw the world's attention to His *Kairos* events - His plan of redemption through the coming and return of Jesus.

These sacred times are summarised in the diagram on the next page to aid you as we discuss each of these cycles further:

1. Sabbath - The first of these sacred times that Israel is to observe is the weekly Sabbath, first seen in the 7 Days of Creation. It points to the 7 millennia or 7,000 years of world history revolving around the coming of Jesus the Greater Light and His return on the Day of the Lord to usher in the Millennial Sabbath rest.

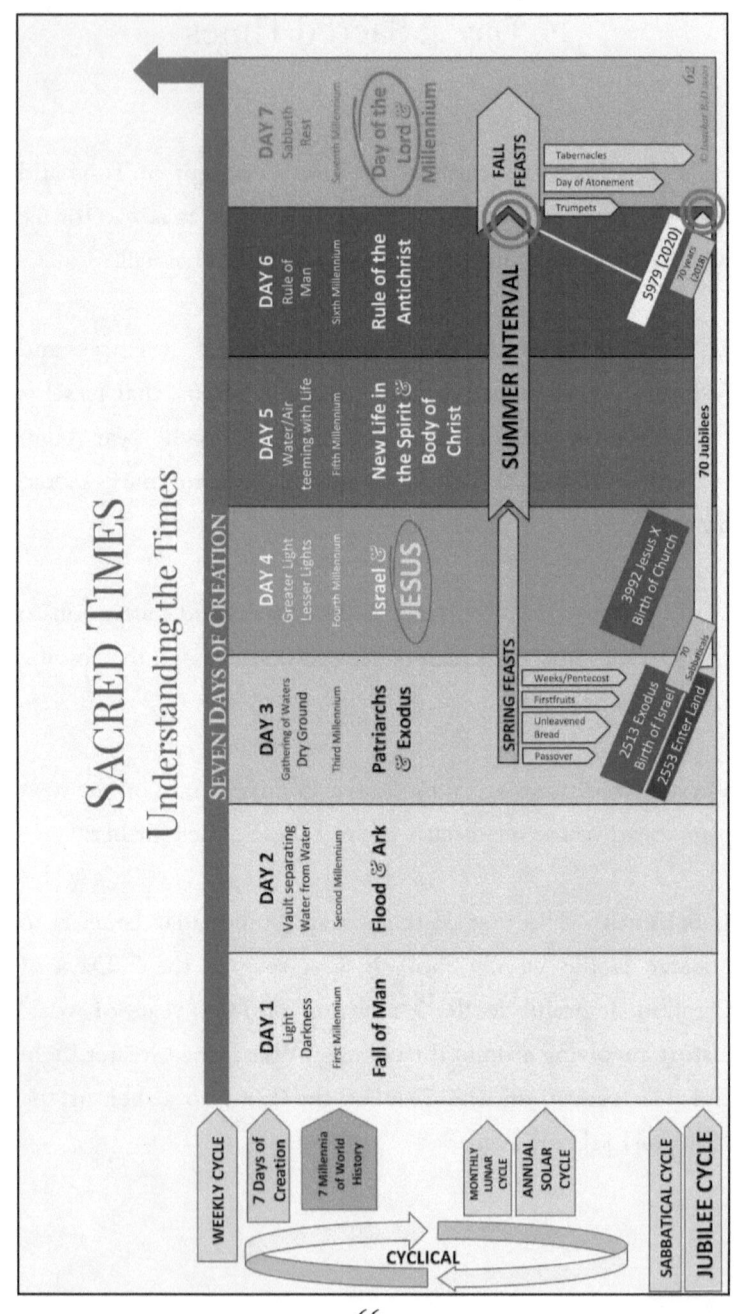

If we understand time as being measured according to the chronology of people and events in the Bible, then **we are reaching the end of the Sixth Millennium** in our day (AD 2020 corresponding to AM 5979 in my calculation). If we go by the narrative of the 7 Days of Creation, God is telling us that the world is living now under the rule of man. One man to be exact - the Antichrist who will soon be revealed in person. The Apostle John tells us in 1 John 4:3 that the spirit of the Antichrist was in fact already at work in our midst since his time.

2. High Sabbath - Besides the weekly Sabbaths, there are 7 Special or High Sabbaths, which can fall on any day of the week, that Israel is to celebrate in the form of 7 Festivals or Feasts of God over 7 months every year. These High Sabbaths, which can be grouped into 4 Spring Feasts and 3 Fall Feasts according to Israel's agricultural calendar, point to 7 *Kairos* events during these 7 millennia of world history.

We know that the Spring Feasts have already been fulfilled in God's *Kairos* 2,000 years ago with Jesus' first coming. Here, the Feasts of Passover, Unleavened Bread and Firstfruits to commemorate the Exodus point to Jesus' sinless or unleavened life, death as our True Passover Lamb, and resurrection as the Firstfruit of the New Creation, opening the way for our salvation and resurrection hope in our exodus from sin. Meanwhile, the birth of Israel as a nation at Mount Sinai, which took place on the Feast of Weeks (also known as

Pentecost) with the giving of the Law, points to the birth of the Church at Mount Zion on the appointed (*Kairos*) Day of Pentecost 1,500 years later with the giving of the Holy Spirit who writes God's Law and eternal covenant on our hearts.

Today, **we are reaching the end of the Summer Interval**, this **Age of Grace** and **Year of the Lord's Favour** (Isaiah 61:1-2a, Luke 4:18-19). This period, better known as the **Church Age**, will be followed in God's *Kairos* by the Fall Feasts when Jesus returns to bring about another great exodus - that of the final deliverance of God's people from His enemies and ultimately from eternal death. We will talk more about the Fall Feasts later.

3. Sabbatical and Jubilee year - Lastly, God commanded Israel to let the land rest every Sabbatical year and to further proclaim freedom for the people during the year of Jubilee. These cycles are to start after Israel enters the Promised Land and point to the spiritual rest and freedom that the world and mankind will finally experience during the Millennial Sabbath after 6,000 years of human sin and struggle.

Historically, the Promised Land only got its rest after 70 Sabbatical cycles, during Israel's exile in Babylon (Leviticus 26:34-35, 2 Chronicles 36:20-21). Today, we are in the 70th Jubilee cycle from the time Israel first entered the Promised Land and the 40th Jubilee cycle since Christ's first coming. After 2,000 years in exile, Israel is now back in the Promised

Land and, interestingly, celebrated in 2018 70 years since its rebirth as a nation in 1948. The Israel we know today is far from God and the Church is not doing that much better - the book of Revelations hints at a similar end time "Babylonian exile" for believers as they struggle to preserve their faith amid the growing apostasy within the Church. All these indicators seem to suggest that **we are in the final Jubilee, the final generation** in God's *Kairos* who will witness Jesus' return to usher in this Millennial rest.

22. Day 4: History of Israel – Part 1 (Israel & Church)

✝

***Through* whom**
***For* whom**
***In* whom**

WE saw how God equipped Israel to be His lesser light pointing us to Jesus through the giving of the Law, Tabernacle, Priesthood, Sacrifices, and Sacred Times. Despite its imperfections, weaknesses and outright disobedience and unfaithfulness, Israel is God's chosen Kingdom through whom Jesus came 2,000 years ago and for whom Jesus will return in the end times.

We also see the Church reflecting the light and life of Jesus, especially for the past 2,000 years from the time of Israel's destruction in AD 70 until its rebirth about 70 years ago in 1948.

That the Church should shine during this period when Israel's light had been put out for the time being is no coincidence but was part of God's plan of salvation from the very beginning, because the Church is God's chosen Kingdom in whom the Body of Christ will reach its full maturity.

Let me explain:

This mystery is that through the gospel the Gentiles are heirs together with Israel, members together of one body, and sharers together in the promise in Christ Jesus ... which for ages past was kept hidden in God, who created all things. His intent was that now, ***through the church, the manifold wisdom of God should be made known***

- Ephesians 3:6-10

We saw earlier how Jacob, in blessing Ephraim, had prophesied that Israel would become a multitude of nations, the fullness of the Gentiles, thus fulfilling God's promise to bless all peoples through Abraham. This came to pass through the Church. Because Israel had rejected Jesus and the Gospel, Paul explains above that the Church has now been tasked to make known this manifold wisdom of God whereby through the Gospel Gentiles are made heirs together with Israel, members together of one body.

Did God's people [Israel] *stumble and fall beyond recovery? Of course not!* ***They were disobedient, so God made salvation available to the Gentiles*** *... some of these branches from Abraham's tree - some of the people of Israel - have been broken off.* ***And you Gentiles, who were branches from a wild olive tree, have been grafted in*** *... I* ***want you to understand this mystery ... so that you will not feel proud about yourselves.*** *Some of the people of Israel have hard hearts, but* ***this will last only until the full number of Gentiles comes to Christ.*** *And so all Israel will be saved* - Romans 11:11-32

But Paul also makes clear above that the Gentiles are being grafted into God's Kingdom of Israel (Abraham's tree) during this period of Israel's disobedience and hardening in part. The largely Gentile Church is not separate from Israel, not distinct from let alone replace Israel as the final or perfected Kingdom of God. It is only here for a season and a purpose:

To be God's light to the world *until the Body of Christ reaches its full maturity* once those who belong to Him among the nations have entered into His Kingdom.

When the full number of Gentiles comes to Christ, God will turn His attention back to Israel even as the Church falls into deception and apostasy, as we will see later.

Now, just as the Gospel and its stewardship under the Church is a perplexing mystery that the Jews find hard to accept to the benefit of Gentiles, Israel's eventual restoration as God's Kingdom that will welcome Jesus' return even as the Church falls into apostasy is an equally perplexing mystery that many of us Christians may find hard to accept. It is indeed a mystery that Paul wants us to understand *"so that you* [Gentiles] *will not feel proud about yourselves."*

In closing, I just want to highlight that the Church - being an ingrafted branch - shares the same DNA as Israel right down to its imperfections, weaknesses and outright disobedience and unfaithfulness. As we will see later, Israel's history would virtually repeat itself in the growth and development of the Church. This is why Paul, in 1 Corinthians 10:11, points out how Israel serves as an "*example*" for the Church. He uses the Greek term *tupos* which means, in the technical sense, a pattern in conformity to which something must be made; in an ethical sense, a warning; and in a doctrinal or Biblical sense, a person or thing prefiguring or foretelling a future person or thing as it relates to Jesus. In other words, Paul is telling us that **what happened to Israel is not only instructive but prophetic of what will come upon the Church**.

23. Day 4: History of Israel – Part 2 (Lessons from the Wilderness)

✝

IN this reading, we will cover the period from the time the Israelites left Mount Sinai until a new generation stood by the banks of the Jordan river 40 years later, and the prophetic lessons we can learn from their wilderness journey.

Warfare Worship Witness

First, when Israel set out to conquer the Promised Land, the nation was effectively entering into warfare as they would need to defeat the pagan peoples occupying the land then. Similarly, the Church is called into warfare and we must expect and be prepared for spiritual opposition as we rescue and take possession of lost souls for God's Kingdom.

Next, the way the Israelites were encamped around the Tabernacle of God as they proceeded on their journey reflected how the life and community of the Israelites then, just as the life and community of the Church today, must revolve around the worship of God as a witness to the surrounding nations. This is our primary weapon to win others to Christ - by reflecting God's glory as His lesser light and so draw people to Him. Worship is also important in warfare as the devil will try to derail us through earthly distractions and temptations or by using fear and intimidation. We can only stand firm and overcome when we keep our focus on God alone. When we worship God in this way and have no other idols before us, we won't give the enemy a foothold in our hearts.

40 - Testing and trials, patient obedience, judgment

A journey that should have lasted 11 days ended up taking 40 long years (Deuteronomy 1:2, Numbers 33). This wilderness period is prophetic of the 40 Jubilees from the time the Church, filled with the Holy Spirit, moved out of the upper room on the Day of Pentecost almost 2,000 years ago until now as this generation, like the one led by Joshua, await Jesus' return to lead us into the Promised Land of His Millennial Kingdom and ultimately into eternity with God.

The number 40 in the Bible is often associated with testing and trials, patient obedience and judgment. Like Moses who was up on the mountain of God for 40 days (Exodus 24:18, 32:1), Jesus is up on the heavenly throne of God these 40 Jubilees, a trial period to test whether we will remain faithful to Him while we wait for His return. We can either be like the rebellious 3,000 who died at Mount Sinai during the first Pentecost, or like the believing 3,000 who were saved at Mount Zion on the Day of Pentecost (Exodus 32:28, Acts 2:41).

Kingship Love Obedience

Ultimately, at the heart of the matter is the matter of the heart. Kingdom life is about God's Kingship over Israel and the Church and the lives of each and every citizen of the Kingdom. It was, is, and will always be about love and obedience. As Jesus Himself puts it, *"If you love Me, keep My commands"* (John 14:15). Obedience should not be out of habit or even duty, which can only fulfill the letter but not the spirit of the Law. It must ultimately stem from a heart of love for God.

24. Day 4: History of Israel – Part 3 (Israel from Yehoshua to Yeshua)

✝

WE saw the importance of kingship, love and obedience in the Kingdom life of God's nation and His people. When we examine Israel's history from the time of Joshua (Yehoshua) to Jesus (Yeshua), we find that failure in precisely these areas was what ultimately led to the country's downfall.

God as King - It didn't start out this way though. Following the Exodus and wilderness years, we are told in Joshua 24:31 that the Israelites under Joshua served God all the days of their lives.

No king - However, when a new generation arose, they neither knew God nor what He had done for Israel. Because they did not acknowledge Him as King and instead worshipped the idols of the peoples around them, God disciplined the Israelites by allowing their enemies to force them to a point of repentance. Each time they cried out to God for help, He was faithful to raise up a judge or leader to deliver them and give them rest from their enemies. The people would remain faithful until that judge died, and then a new generation would arise to repeat this vicious cycle. The book of Judges sums it up with the statement, *"In those days Israel had no King; everyone did as they saw fit"* (Judges 17:6, 18:1, 19:1, 21:25).

Human king - Despite 3 centuries of going through the same cycle of idolatry, oppression, repentance and deliverance, the Israelites still did not acknowledge God as their True King. Instead, they longed to be like the nations around them and demanded for a human king.

Israel existed as a united kingdom for 120 years and reached its peak in the early years of King Solomon's rule. When Solomon completed the First Temple in Jerusalem in AM 3000 - the beginning of Day 4 or the Fourth Millennium - Israel was finally fully equipped to serve as God's lesser light drawing all nations to worship Him at His holy mountain. But this was not to be. Unlike his father David who was after God's own heart, Solomon loved women more than he loved God. This eventually led to idolatry with disastrous consequences for the nation. Israel will only recover its former glory when Jesus returns to rule from Mount Zion during the Millennium.

But for now, the once united and powerful kingdom became divided and severely weakened after Solomon's death. Both the Northern Kingdom of Israel and the Southern Kingdom of Judah became vulnerable to foreign powers, tempted to make compromises and fell into idolatry, corruption and injustice. Both rejected the warnings of God's Prophets as we will see later.

Division and exile - God eventually punished and exiled the 2 Jewish kingdoms for their sins - Israel to Assyria in 722 BC and Judah to Babylon in 586 BC. The land rested for 70 years during the Babylonian exile to make up for all the years that Israel did not keep the Sabbatical and Jubilee cycles. God disciplined Israel but also set a definite time frame after which He would restore His people and deal with His enemies.

Restoration and return - So in His *Kairos* in 538 BC, God released His *Rhema* - amazingly through the pagan king Cyrus, who issued a proclamation allowing the Jews to return to the Promised Land to rebuild Jerusalem and the Temple. And in His *Kairos* about 530-plus years after that, God Himself would come to His people as a man, the *Logos* made flesh - Jesus the Greater Light, *Messiah* ben Joseph, the Lamb of God and Saviour of the World.

25. Day 4: History of Israel – Part 4 (Church – Commonwealth of Israel)

✝

WHEN we compare the histories of Israel and the Church, the Commonwealth of Israel (Ephesians 2:12), we see a remarkable prophetic parallel between them (see next page).

God as King - First, the generation during the time of the 12 Apostles mirrored the Joshua generation. There was general faithfulness to God - the Church under the leadership of the Apostles and elders who witnessed Jesus' acts firsthand; Israel under the leadership of Joshua and the elders who witnessed God's acts firsthand.

No king - Next, the era of the Early Church Fathers. This period was similar to the era of the Judges in that there was *"no king"* - no central scriptural authority defining what was Biblically or doctrinally correct, just as there was no central political authority in Israel then defining what was legally or morally correct. The Bible as we know it today was not decided upon until the Fifth Century. Consequently, everyone *"did what was right in their own eyes"* when it came to God's Word, resulting in a cycle of false teachings and doctrines, convening of church councils to fight these errors, and a return to doctrinal truth until the next heresy hit, not unlike the cycles that defined the period of the Judges.

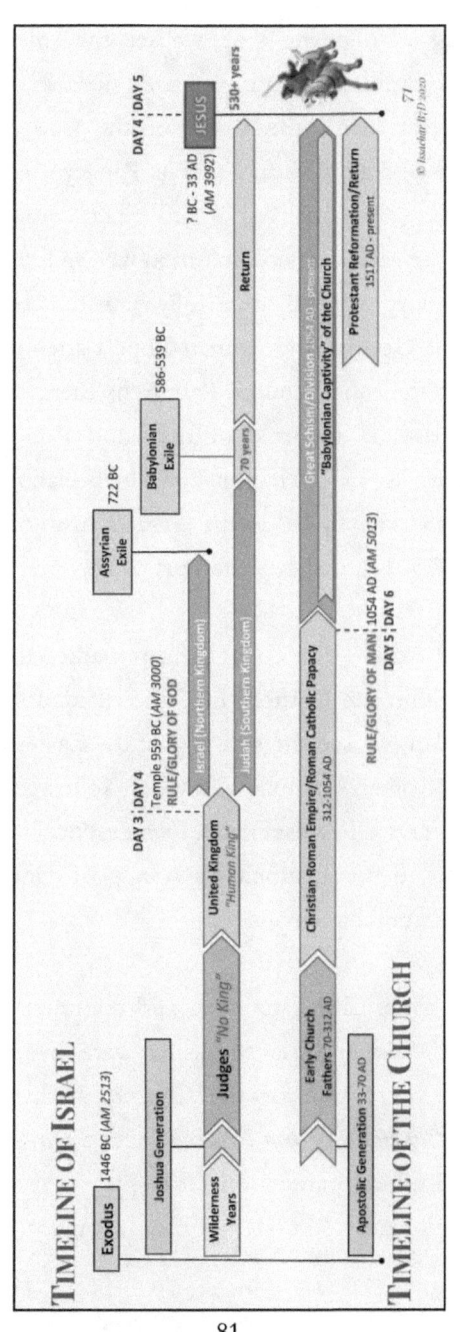

Human king - Following that, we see the emergence of a human king combining both political, worldly power and spiritual authority with the dawn of the Christian Roman Empire and rise of the Roman Catholic Papacy.

But while in the early years of Solomon we see Israel reflecting the rule and glory of God most fully with the completion of the Temple of God, in the Roman Pope's attempt to elevate himself above the other Church Patriarchs then, we see in the Church the rise of the rule of man and a monument or institution built to his own glory. We will elaborate on this later. This act ultimately led to the Great Schism or division of AD 1054 (AM 5013), marking the start of Day 6.

Division and exile - The Great Schism marked the beginning of division within the Church. Like the divided kingdoms of Israel and Judah, we see the splitting of the Eastern Orthodox and Western Roman Catholic Churches, followed by Roman Catholicism and Protestantism, emergence of various denominations, denominational vs non/post-denominational, charismatic vs non-charismatic etc.

At the same time, Christians were and continue to be taken into spiritual exile and slavery as it were by the growing apostasy and corruption of the Church. In his work ***The Babylonian Captivity of the Church*** written almost 500 years ago, Martin Luther pointed out that just as the Jews were carried away from Jerusalem into captivity under the oppression of the Babylonian Empire, so in Europe during his time Christians had been carried away from the Scriptures and made subject to the power of the Roman Catholic Papacy through various unscriptural practices. This spread of deception and misuse of religious authority throughout the worldwide Church will only grow more and more as we reach the end of Day 6 with the revealing of the Antichrist.

Restoration and return - But just as God restored the faithful among the Jews after a season of discipline, He restores the faithful among the Church in His *Kairos*. As in the days of Cyrus, God released His *Rhema* through Luther's proclamation of the basic doctrines of faith, grace and Scripture alone. This triggered the beginning of the return of God's people back to His Truth as found in the Bible with the Protestant Reformation of 1517, something that continues even today amidst the growing darkness both in the Church and in the world until the full number of Gentiles has entered the Kingdom.

And then, in His *Kairos* on the Day of the Lord, God Himself will return as Jesus, *Messiah* ben Judah, the Lion of Judah, King of Kings and Lord of Lords. *"Amen. Come, Lord Jesus"* (Revelations 22:20)!

26. Day 4: Signs of the Times
†

*The Pharisees and Sadducees came to Jesus and tested Him by asking Him to show them a sign from heaven. He replied ... "You know how to interpret the appearance of the sky, but you cannot interpret the **signs of the times**. A wicked and adulterous **generation** looks for a sign, but none will be given it except the **sign of Jonah**." Jesus then left them and went away* - Matthew 16:1-4

AT this point, I want us to consider the various signs of the times found in our study of God's Word so far. This is because we are called to understand these signs and not be like the hypocritical religious leaders in Jesus' time seen above who were not satisfied with those signs already given to them but demanded more. Ultimately, such individuals will never be convinced and will face the consequences of their unbelief.

1. We are reaching the end of the Sixth Millennium (AD 2020/AM 5979). For Jews, the year is AM 5780 but given that there may be 165 missing years in their calendar (we don't have time to get into this here), the correct Jewish year could be AM 5945 - which is close to our own calculations.

2. We are reaching the end of the Summer Interval - The Spring Feasts were fulfilled with Jesus' first coming and birth of the Church. It is no coincidence that the Jewish nation ceased to exist shortly thereafter, as this was part of God's plan for the Church to act as His lesser light during this Age of

Grace and Year of the Lord's Favour to gather in the summer harvest of the fullness of the Gentiles. But now that Israel has been reborn, we can expect God to turn His attention back to His chosen Kingdom who will welcome Jesus' return in fulfilment of the Fall Feasts.

3. We are in the final Jubilee cycle - The 70th Jubilee cycle since the Israelites entered the Promised Land and 40th Jubilee cycle since Jesus' first coming and birth of the Church. Interestingly, in 2018, Israel also celebrated 70 years of nationhood. Now, each Jubilee cycle is 49/50 years.

Besides the above signs, in 2017, the Protestant Church celebrated 500 years since Luther's proclamation. If Jesus first came 530-plus years after Cyrus' proclamation, going by this same time-frame, we could be left with 30-plus years before He returns. This fits in with our other indicators, **all pointing to the next 20-50 years or so**.

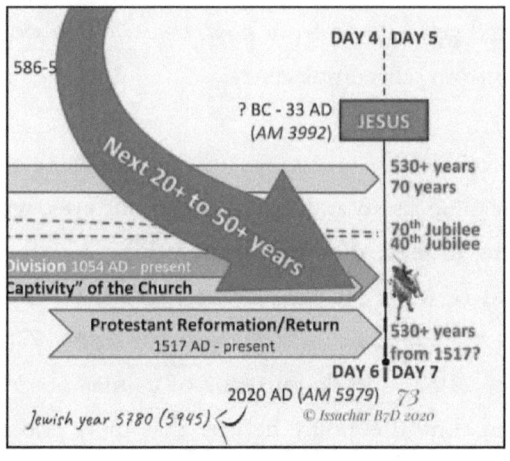

Now learn this lesson from the fig tree: As soon as its twigs get tender and its leaves come out, you know that summer is near. Even so, **when you see all these things, you know that it is near, right at the door.** *Truly I tell you,* **this generation** *will certainly not pass away until all these things have happened* - Matthew 24:32-34

Now, some of you may object - did Jesus Himself not say that we will not know when He will return? That even He doesn't know - only the Father knows - and that His coming will be like a thief in the night? I will address this in detail at the end of this book but at this point I just want to say that what we are doing here does not contradict Jesus' words. We are not here to figure out exactly when Jesus is coming, to pinpoint the exact date of His return. But as the verses above suggest, **we are expected to understand the signs of the times so that we know how near we are to His coming**. Knowing how near is different from knowing the exact date, but it is also very different from saying that it could be now, in this generation, or a hundred generations from now, because that would make us wake up from our complacency.

So if we stop closing our minds to the timeframe that these signs are leading us to and instead open our eyes, we will see that **we are indeed the final generation**. We are the ones Jesus speaks of when He says, *"Truly I tell you, this generation will certainly not pass away until all these things have happened"* (Matthew 24:34, Luke 21:32). No doubt many of us may not live to see this happen, but the point here is that there will be those among us even now who will witness the events leading to Jesus' return.

*A wicked and adulterous generation asks for a sign! But none will be given it except the **sign of the prophet Jonah** ... The men of Nineveh will stand up at the judgment with **this generation** and condemn it; for they repented at the preaching of Jonah, and now something greater than Jonah is here* - Matthew 12:38-42

Jesus speaks of the sign of Jonah more than once. In the verses above, He explains that this sign refers to His death and resurrection. But Jesus also mentions how, ironically, the men of Nineveh - Israel's enemy - repented at Jonah's preaching, while God's own people did not receive Jesus, the very *Logos* or Word of God. Consequently, while the Ninevites were spared from God's judgment which was to come 40 days later (Jonah 3:4), for these unbelieving Jews, their end did come within their generation about 40 years later with the Roman exile.

Today, we are that generation to whom the sign of Jonah is once again given for a final time. We can choose to repent and believe like the Ninevites or continue ignoring the meaning of this and all the other signs I have listed here like the Jews of Jesus' day - until it is too late.

27. Day 4: Reflections - For Such a Time as This

✝

*"For if you remain silent at this time, relief and deliverance for the Jews will arise from another place, but you and your father's family will perish. And **who knows but that you have come to your royal position for such a time as this?**" Then Esther sent this reply to Mordecai: … "I will go to the king, even though it is against the law. And **if I perish, I perish**"* - Esther 4:14-16

THE book of Esther is unique in that there is no mention of God inside. Yet God's hand is clearly at work through a young Jewish girl who had the courage to stand and speak His *Rhema* in His *Kairos*. As a result, God's people were rescued from total destruction.

The evil in Esther's time is the same evil that wiped out 6 million Jews during the Jewish Holocaust of World War II. It is a solemn reminder that God's enemies, led by Satan, will not stop seeking to destroy God's people until Jesus returns in judgment. Even now, the world is lining up against Israel, while Christian communities are being persecuted everywhere. We are told that an end-time holocaust will come when *"all who refused to worship the image* [of Satan] *"* will be killed (Revelations 13:15). Our Lord Himself has already warned us of what is to come, *"Then you will be handed over to be persecuted and put to death, and you will be hated by all nations because of Me"* (Matthew 24:9).

The enemy's attacks are also being carried out within the Church as apostasy grows and God's Truth is undermined. We are that generation that will not only see Jesus' return to bring in the dawn of a glorious new millennium but to live through the darkest of the darkest nights before it.

As mentioned earlier, the purpose of the ***Issachar B7D Fellowship*** is not to speculate on dates but to understand the signs of the times so that we know how close we are to Jesus' return. More importantly, we are called to know not just for the sake of knowing, but so that we know what to do in such times. For the past 2,000 years, we have heard and heeded God's *Rhema* in the form of the Great Commission. This must continue until the full number of Gentiles has entered the Kingdom. But we are now living in the last Jubilee. We are that final generation whom Jesus is speaking to in Matthew 24. It is time to recognise that the signs point to us, and that we should therefore hear and respond to His *Rhema* for us in this *Kairos*.

Repair Rebuild Rescue

Like Ezra and Nehemiah, we are called to repair the foundations and rebuild the walls of our faith, both individually and together as one people of God, so that we will survive when the storms of internal apostasy and external persecution hit. Like Esther, we are to rescue His people, not just by bringing them into the faith but to help them hang on to it until Jesus returns.

As the opening passage tells us, God's work and will can never be undermined, despite our inaction or even outright disobedience. As Mordecai puts it, *"if you remain silent at this time, relief and deliverance for the Jews will arise from another place."* God doesn't need us, but He did choose us so that we have the privilege and joy of participating in His divine plan. May those who see the signs and hear God's *Rhema* as we do persevere with the kind of faith and courage that Mordecai and Esther, Ezra and Nehemiah, had. After all, *"who knows but that you have come to your ... position for such a time as this?"*

28. Day 4: Prophets
✝

SO far, we learnt of God's purpose for Israel His lesser light to indirectly point us to Jesus and pave the way for His coming and return. But God didn't stop at just that. He spoke plainly to His people and to all mankind about Jesus through His Prophets.

The table on the next page lists the 16 Prophets whose writings make up the Old Testament prophetic books. It shows the era in which they prophesied and the nations they mainly directed their messages to. We can also locate this 400-year period of the Prophets against our earlier timeline of Israel. Interestingly, 400 years of silence would pass after this period before John the Baptist arrives on the scene to announce the coming of Jesus.

These Prophets, who guided and warned the Israelites in their walk with God throughout Israel's history, proclaimed God's *Rhema* in His *Kairos* that **a *Messiah* or Anointed One would come to establish His Kingdom on earth**.

And then, in God's *Kairos*, His Word literally came to life in Jesus, who died for our sins to fulfill His *Rhema* as spoken of in the Law and through these Prophets.

PROPHETS OF THE OLD TESTAMENT

PERIOD	TO JUDAH	TO ISRAEL	TO OTHERS
Early History of the Divided Kingdom (930-760 BC)	Joel (c. 820 BC?)		Obadiah (c. 840-825 BC?) - to Edom Jonah (c. 800-750 BC) - to Assyria
Assyrian Age (760-627 BC)	Isaiah (740-690 BC) Micah (c. 735-700 BC)	Amos (c. 760-750 BC) Hosea (c. 760-730 BC) Fall of Samaria (722)	
Babylonian Age I (627-586 BC)	Zephaniah (c. 627 BC) Jeremiah (626-586 BC) Habakkuk (c. 605 BC) Fall of Jerusalem (586 BC)		Nahum (c. 627 BC) - to Assyria
Babylonian Age II (586-539 BC)	Daniel (605-537 BC) Ezekiel (593-571 BC)		
Persian Age (538-330 BC)	Rebuilding of Temple (538-516 BC) Haggai (520 BC) Zechariah (520-518 BC) Malachi (433 BC)		

Period of the Prophets (840–433 BC)

Assyrian Exile — 722 BC
Babylonian Exile — 586-539 BC
70 years — Return

Israel (Northern Kingdom)
Judah (Southern Kingdom)

> *In reading this, then, you will be able to understand my insight into the mystery of* [the Gospel of] *Christ,* ***which was not made known to people in other generations as it has now*** [*Kairos*] ***been revealed*** [*Rhema*] *by the Spirit to God's holy apostles and prophets*
> - Ephesians 3:4-5

Following His resurrection, Jesus commanded His Apostles to proclaim the **Gospel or Good News that He is the *Messiah* and His Kingdom has arrived** and so make disciples of all nations - although for now, His Kingdom remains hidden in the hearts of His people as they await His return. Since then, every generation of the Church has reached out into the world to fulfill this Great Commission. Paul tells us above that this has been God's *Rhema* in this *Kairos* period of His grace, kept hidden previously but revealed to the Apostles and the Church.

Now, we are standing at the end of history, almost 2,000 years since Jesus first came. We saw previously how we are very likely the last generation, the ones who will experience the end-time tribulation and finally witness Jesus' return.

In this *Kairos* moment, God is once again releasing His *Rhema* to His people, kept hidden previously but now revealed through the signs of the times as understood in light of the 7 Days of Creation, which is to proclaim that **Jesus the *Messiah* and His Kingdom will soon return**. His Kingdom will no longer be confined within the hearts of people. Instead, Jesus will set up His Millennial Kingdom to rule over the earth from

His throne in Jerusalem, and Israel will be restored to fulfill its destiny as His Kingdom of priests and holy nation.

The following summarises how Israel and the Church serve as God's lesser lights pointing us to Jesus the Greater Light.

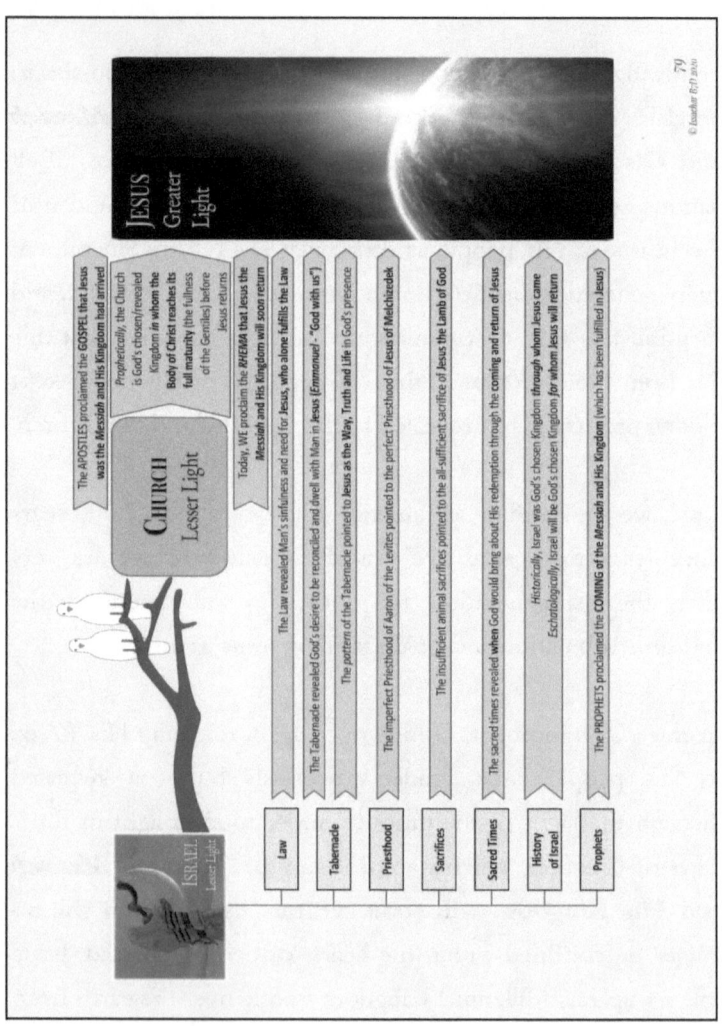

29. Day 4: Prophetic Narrative & *Rhema* – Part 1 (Understanding the Message)

✝

WE saw how God had progressively released His *Rhema* in His *Kairos* - first to the Old Testament Prophets, then to the Apostles and the Church, and now to those of us who recognise the signs of the times. These are not 3 separate messages but a single unified voice or prophetic narrative concerning Jesus' first coming and His soon return.

I want to make 3 important observations:

1. Not a new message - First, this message that we are now called to proclaim is not something new to the Word of God, like a new book or chapter in addition to what has already been written in the Bible. The Bible warns us not to add to or subtract from God's Word. It is a message that had been there all along, only that it was hidden in the Scriptures in various signs and symbols, peoples and events throughout the Bible, as we have seen for ourselves here.

*"Go your way, Daniel, because **the words are rolled up and sealed until the time of the end** ... None of the wicked will understand, but **those who are wise will understand**"* - Daniel 12:9-10

> *For **we know in part** and **we prophesy in part**, but when completeness comes, what is in part disappears ... For **now we see through a glass, darkly**; but then face to face: now I know in part; but then shall I know even as also I am known* - 1 Corinthians 13:12

God's messengers in the past had in fact hinted at its existence as seen in the verses above. Even as they prophesied and declared those things that were made known to them, they pointed to something more and the incompleteness of their own understanding.

> [Jesus] *said to them, "Therefore every teacher of the law who has become a disciple in the kingdom of heaven is like the owner of a house **who brings out of his storeroom new treasures as well as old***"
> - Matthew 13:52

2. Yet a new message - Having said this however, this message is new in that what was hidden before - the Bible uses the term "mystery" - has now been made known to us in God's *Kairos*.

Jesus speaks about this in the verse above. During His time, God's Word only consisted of the Old Testament, also known as the Law and Prophets. This was because the rest of the Bible - the New Testament - had yet to be written. However, Jesus said that when those who taught God's Word became His disciples, they would find in the "*storeroom*" of the Old Testament not just the "*old treasures*" of what they already knew, but "*new treasures*" of mysteries and things unknown to them previously which were now made known and explained to them by God's revelation.

The Apostle Paul is the best example of this.

Paul used to possess only the old treasures of the Law and Prophets as a devout Pharisee or Jewish religious teacher. But following his conversion to Christianity on the road to Damascus, God opened Paul's eyes and understanding to see the new treasures of 2 greatest mysteries hidden in the Old Testament - that of the Gospel of Jesus Christ and the mystery of the Church opening the way for Gentiles to enter into God's Kingdom. Paul's writings, which concern mainly these 2 mysteries, make up almost half of the New Testament books.

Today, we are privileged to be that generation who will find in the Bible not just the old treasures of what has already been taught, the doctrines that make up our Christian faith, but also new treasures concerning the final mysteries surrounding the end times. As the final generation before Jesus returns, God wants us to understand the signs of the times, know the nearness of His return, recognise the trials that will arise, and therefore prepare and equip ourselves and others for what needs to be done - but only if we believe and receive God's *Rhema* that is being released today.

3. This message is the climax - Lastly, this message completes the entire picture, the culmination of a common prophetic narrative. As mentioned earlier, the Old Testament Prophets addressed various nations over a period of 400 years, bringing God's *Rhema* to His people as well as His enemies. Yet there was a common theme or narrative shared by these Prophets that would only be partially fulfilled during their time, nor was it completely fulfilled at the first coming of Jesus or during the time of the Apostles, but pointed to a distant future, a future that is now upon us, when God will bring about its eventual and complete fulfilment.

The thought of prophecies having partial and multiple gradual fulfilments should not surprise us given our earlier cyclical understanding of time. This idea is best reflected in the Jewish word for "year" (*Shanah*). It shares the same root as the words "repeat" and "change" portraying time as an ascending helix, where there is a repeat or review of key historical events - in other words, history and prophecy repeating itself - but also change brought about by the multiple gradual fulfilment of prophecy.

Further, the prophetic narrative that we will be looking at in greater detail at different points in this book applies not only to Israel but also the Church. As we had learnt previously, what befell Israel was not only instructive but prophetic of what would come upon the Church as the Commonwealth of Israel during this period of grace.

30. Day 4: Prophetic Narrative & *Rhema* – Part 2 (Discipline vs Judgment)

✝

LET us now outline the common prophetic narrative running through the messages of the Old Testament Prophets.

1. God's discipline and exile of His people - First, the Prophets warned the kingdoms of Israel and Judah that God would soon discipline and exile His people. Instead of worshipping and trusting in God alone to protect the nation, both kingdoms chased after the idols of their neighbours and relied on external political alliances for survival. There was division and infighting within and between the 2 divided kingdoms, as well as widespread corruption and social injustice. Most of all, the Israelites had forsaken their mission as God's lesser light to the world. As the end approached, there was widespread deception and many false prophets emerged who misled the people by promising peace or at most a short exile, instead of repenting of their sins and turning back to God.

All that the Prophets foretold eventually came to pass during the Assyrian and Babylonian exiles. This pattern of discipline and exile would take place again to Israel under the Romans in Jesus' time after they rejected Him, an exile that would last 2,000 years this time round. Although Israel has been reborn since 1948 in fulfilment of prophecy, it is currently a secular nation and will once again come under God's discipline during the Tribulation before it finally acknowledges Jesus as its *Messiah*.

As mentioned before, the warnings of the Prophets also apply to the Church. We saw earlier how Christians have been taken into spiritual exile and slavery as it were by apostasy and corruption within the Church. The condition of the Church will only grow worse as we near the end. Like Israel, the Church is equally guilty of breaking the commandments to love God and man. There is widespread idolatry, division, infighting and injustice. Even today, many Christians are held captive by oppressive human doctrines and superstitions, while others suffer real persecution. Yet those who are spared for now, like their Jewish brothers in the past, remained caught up with materialistic pursuits during this brief period of peace and prosperity and forgot their core mission to be God's light to the world. Instead of heeding God's *Rhema* which is being proclaimed even now and repenting, their ears itch for the lies of false teachers promising endless "blessings" of health, wealth and happiness. They ignore warnings of the coming persecution and exile that will be God's means to discipline and refine His people until it is too late.

For it is time for judgment to begin with God's household; *and if it begins with us, what will the outcome be for those who do not obey the gospel of God?* - 1 Peter 4:17

2. God's sovereignty over and judgment of His enemies - That the Prophets should reprimand their own countrymen first is not surprising. Peter speaks above of how God's judgment will begin with His own people. But the Prophets also recognised that God is sovereign and will eventually judge His enemies. It is God who stirred up the ancient empires from Egypt, Assyria and Babylon to Medo-Persia, Greece and Rome, as well as Israel's pagan neighbours, to act as His instruments to test and discipline His people. However, when their time was up, God in turn brought about their eventual judgment for their wickedness and cruelty. The words of the Prophets were all fulfilled with the judgment and fall of every single one of these empires, the last being the Roman Empire in AD 476.

Now, there are many passages in the Old Testament concerning Israel and its enemies that have yet to be fulfilled. As we near the end of the Sixth Day of Creation and Jesus' soon return, we can expect all these remaining prophecies to come to pass.

We are told, especially by the Prophet Daniel, that a demonic kingdom of man will emerge to try to destroy and replace God's Kingdom on earth. Like its predecessors, this revived Roman-Babylonian Empire will come against Israel as it rallies many nations behind it in an attempt to rule the world. We already see this beginning to happen on the world stage. Its ultimate goal is to lead a worldwide rebellion against Jesus Himself.

And just like how the divided kingdoms of Judah and Israel tried to strike deals and compromises with their neighbours and enemies alike instead of running to God, modern-day Israel and the increasingly apostate Church will do likewise with the nations of this world and ultimately with this evil empire itself. As with these 2 kingdoms, there will also be a brief period of false peace, a lull before the storm.

I draw this connection between the past and future because Judah and Israel are prophetic of modern-day Israel and the Church. Let me explain. The nation of Israel has usually been associated with Judah alone, because it was the exiles from Judah that returned from Babylon to resettle the Promised Land. Judah can also be said to be the legitimate kingdom, the True Israel of God, because it is home to Jerusalem and the royal line of King David and Jesus. The Church meanwhile is an ingrafted kingdom like the Northern Kingdom of Israel. Just as God tore away the 10 tribes of Israel out of Solomon's hand and gave it to Jeroboam (1 Kings 11:30-32), God tore away part of the kingdom from the hands of the Jews and gave it to the predominantly Gentile Church for a season.

Now for many of us, especially among the Protestant Churches, the idea that the Church will turn apostate and depart from God, like the idolatrous Northern Kingdom of Israel, is very hard to accept. Isn't the Church the eternal Bride of Christ? At most, we believe that it must refer to some other "church" and not our own. In fact, we won't even consider them as true churches at all.

But that is precisely it. These institutional branches of the Church - the same earthly universal Church that we are all a part of - have become deformed to the point that we don't even recognise them as belonging to the one Body of Christ. But as the end draws nearer and darkness grows, so will the remaining branches of the Church suffer the same fate as the disease and rot of apostasy spreads. It is only the true believers and children of God regardless of which church they come from who will be made ready, often through the fires of apostasy and persecution, for the Wedding Feast of the Lamb. **This is the mystery of the end-time Church - "*Mystery Babylon*" as John described in the book of Revelations** (see diagram on next page).

In God's *Kairos*, this satanic Roman-Babylonian Empire will eventually betray its true colours. The false promise of world unity and peace will turn out to be a lie as division and war looms. This evil kingdom of man will turn against Israel and the Apostate Church and war against rival nations, as it strives to put its mark and authority on all mankind. As it crumbles and falls in its own wickedness, it will make a last ditch attempt to invade and destroy Israel, setting the stage for the next pivotal scene - the Day of the Lord.

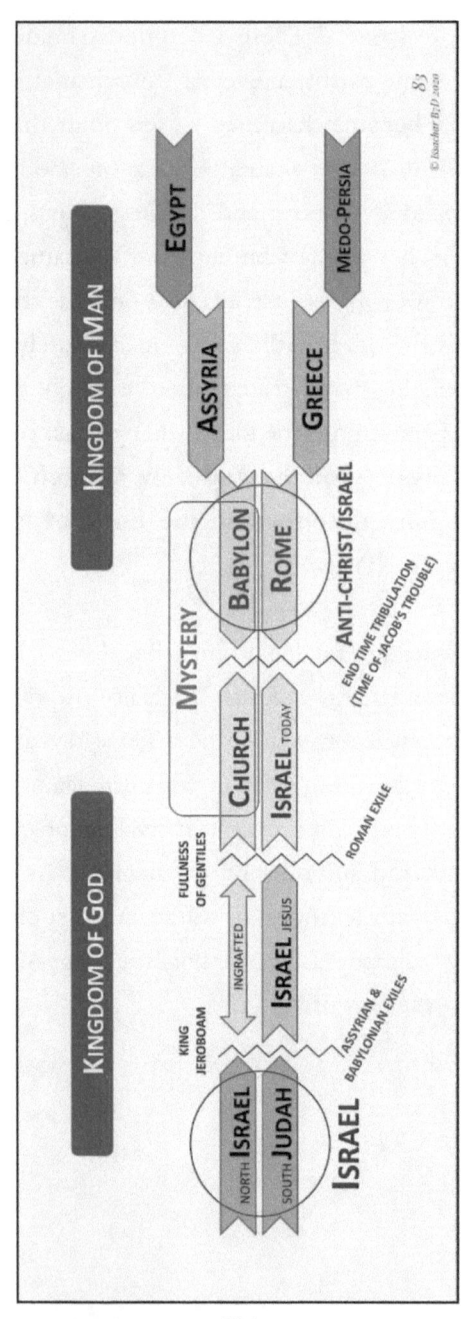

31. Day 4: Prophetic Narrative & *Rhema* – Part 3 (Day of the Lord & Coming of the *Messiah*)

✝

Great and glorious day?
Or dreadful - a day of decision and darkness?

3. DAY of the Lord - This is something mentioned by many of the Old Testament Prophets. It refers to the end of the world as we know it. To the Jews, it is that great day when the *Messiah* will come to deliver Israel from its enemies and usher in His eternal rule. To Christians, it is the glorious Second Coming of Jesus.

Yet the Prophets describe it as a dreadful day, because it is when God's discipline of His wayward people and judgment of His wicked enemies will reach their climax. It is the day when Jesus will return to put an end to the Antichrist's last-ditch attempt to destroy Israel in the Kidron Valley outside Jerusalem, also known as the Valley of Decision. On that day, God will decide who are truly His. Like the Jewish day that begins at sunset, it will be a day that starts in darkness first before giving way to the glorious dawn of Jesus' Millennial rule. Jesus Himself tells us that He will return like a "*thief in the night*" (Matthew 24:43, Revelations 16:15). Be careful what we wish for because we may not be ready for it!

But take heart!

4. Even as God's judgment unfolds, there is comfort, hope and restoration - Even as God's judgment unfolds for His enemies, there is ultimately comfort, hope and restoration for God's people following His discipline. We saw this in the past, and will see it again in the future.

In God's *Kairos*, a faithful remnant of Jews returned from exile to rebuild the nation and the Temple, preparing the way for Jesus' first coming. Through Jesus' death and resurrection, the way of salvation and restoration was open to all mankind.

Now in these last of the last days, God once again brought about the return and regathering of the Jews in 1948. After a time of discipline during the Tribulation, Israel will finally acknowledge its *Messiah* when Jesus returns and be fully restored as His Kingdom on earth during the Millennium and into eternity. The Church, which experienced a partial restoration since the Reformation, will also be comforted with this blessed hope of final and eternal restoration as the Bride of Christ in the New Heaven, Earth and Jerusalem.

5. Central to these, prophecy of the *Messiah* and His Kingdom rule - Central to the entire narrative of the Old Testament Prophets is their prophecy of the *Messiah* as the Suffering Servant and Redeemer at His First Coming, before He returns on the Day of the Lord as the future King of Kings and Lord of Lords - Jesus Christ.

There are at least 353 Old Testament prophecies that have already been fulfilled by Jesus at His first coming. We can be sure that He will fulfill the rest when He returns. In fact, all creation and history, and God's plan and purposes as revealed in the Bible, are about Jesus.

"Destroy this Temple, and I will raise it again in three days." ... the Temple [Jesus] *had spoken of was His body* - John 2:18-21

May the same be said of our lives each day - how we think and live, as well as our perspectives and priorities. May Jesus not only be our Saviour and Redeemer but also our Lord and King, reigning on the throne of our hearts, the only one whom we love with all our heart, soul and mind. As seen above, Jesus is not only our Ark who rescues us from eternal judgment, but our Temple that commands our wholehearted devotion.

I will send My messenger, who will prepare the way before Me. Then suddenly the Lord you are seeking will come to His Temple
- Malachi 3:1

The last few Prophets of the Old Testament (Haggai, Zechariah and Malachi) urged the exiles to finish rebuilding the Temple because, as the verse above tells us, the *Messiah's* coming will be very much linked to the Temple's existence. God will also send a messenger to prepare the way before Him, and yet we are told that His coming will be sudden and unexpected.

This was exactly what happened when Jesus first came. Although announced by John the Baptist and accompanied by various signs and wonders, the people still rejected and crucified Jesus. The Temple in Jesus' time was the most magnificent as it had ever been, but tragically the people totally missed recognising their God, their True Temple. As in the past, God will again send another messenger - in fact, He will send Two Witnesses - to announce Jesus' return. But let us not wait until then to believe that Jesus is indeed returning soon, for the message is already being announced to us now. May we rebuild our spiritual temple and Body of Christ in such a way that we will recognise and be ready to receive our King and not be caught asleep by His sudden return.

32. Day 4: Reflections – Gift of Prophecy
✝

AS we wrap up our journey through the Old Testament Prophets, let us reflect on this highly misunderstood and misused gift, especially in this day and age of lies and deception - the gift of prophecy.

*Follow the way of love and **eagerly desire gifts of the Spirit, especially prophecy.** For anyone who speaks in a tongue does not speak to people but to God. Indeed, no one understands them; they utter mysteries by the Spirit. But **the one who prophesies speaks to people for their strengthening, encouraging and comfort.** Anyone who speaks in a tongue edifies themselves, but **the one who prophesies edifies the church*** - 1 Corinthians 14:1-4

Paul tells us that prophecy is a spiritual gift that we should especially *"eagerly desire."* The Greek word for prophecy (*Propheteuo*) used here more accurately means to "speak forth by divine inspiration" - in other words, to proclaim God's *Rhema* in His *Kairos*.

Forth-telling *vs* fore-telling

Many think prophecy is about predicting the future. While it can carry this meaning and some prophecies do contain a predictive element, the spiritual gift of prophecy is mainly a gift of proclamation or "forth-telling," not prediction or "fore-telling."

Repair Rebuild Rescue ... *Release*

Earlier, we learnt that the purpose of the *Issachar B7D Fellowship* is to repair, rebuild and rescue.

Here, we are further called to release God's Word to His people - to prophesy to those whom the Lord calls by proclaiming His *Rhema* in His *Kairos*, which is NOW. It is not about predicting the future, when Christ will return. It is about speaking forth about the present, understanding the signs of the times and in so doing knowing what God wants us to do. As Paul puts it here, the purpose of prophecy is to "*strengthen*" (our resolve to act), "*encourage*" (us to keep going when we face obstacles and trials), and "*comfort*" (us when we suffer because of our obedience to Jesus). It is to "*edify the church.*" God's *Rhema* is meant to stir us into action as one Body of Christ, to preserve the faith of our brothers and sisters until Jesus returns.

We can expect ridicule and persecution, even from within the Church. Jesus said, "*Remember what I told you: 'A servant is not greater than his master.' If they persecuted Me, they will persecute you also … 'I have told you these things, so that in Me you may have peace. In this world you will have trouble. But take heart! I have overcome the world*" (Jn 15:20, 16:33). We have already been warned. May God give us the conviction, character and courage to take up the Cross of Christ and follow Him.

33. Day 4: Jesus Christ – Man

✝

And beginning with Moses and all the Prophets, [Jesus] *explained to them what was said in all the Scriptures concerning Himself*
- Luke 24:25-27

TURNING now to the New Testament, we begin here with a most challenging task, for who can adequately describe Jesus Christ our great and awesome Lord and Saviour? As we recall some of the key truths we have learnt so far about Jesus (as well as others that we did not have the time to cover), I wonder if our list below matches that of our Lord's when He explained to the disciples who were on the way to Emmaus what was said in all the Scriptures concerning Himself.

Jesus is God.

Jesus is the Word (*Logos*) made flesh. He is the *Rhema* through whom God spoke Time and Creation into being and is also the fullest revelation of God to Man (Hebrews 1:1-3).

Jesus is the Alpha and Omega, the Beginning and the End (Revelations 1:8, 21:6, 22:13). He existed before Time and will bring Creation into eternal *Shalom* in Him.

Jesus is the True Light foreshadowed in the First Day of Creation that drives out all darkness.

Although Jesus is God, He is also fully human. He is the True Son of Man promised to Adam and Eve immediately after the Fall to crush the head of Satan.

Jesus is the True Noah bringing us everlasting comfort and rest, the True Ark that lifts us out of the flood of God's final judgment foreshadowed in the Second Day of Creation.

Jesus is the True Dry Ground that rescues us out of the sea of sin and death foreshadowed in the Third Day of Creation.

Jesus is the Fulfilment of God's covenant with Abraham, Isaac and Jacob.

Jesus is the True Isaac, the True Son of Promise.

Jesus is the True Jacob, the first among the elect or chosen of God.

Jesus is the Promised *Messiah* spoken of in the prophetic names of the 10 generations from Adam to Noah and the 12 Tribes of Israel.

Jesus is *Messiah* ben Joseph the suffering Lamb of God and *Messiah* ben Judah the victorious Lion of Judah.

Jesus is both King and Priest foreshadowed by King Melchizedek of ancient Jerusalem.

Jesus is the True Moses, leading us out of bondage and slavery to sin.

Jesus is the Blood of the True Firstborn sacrificed so that God's judgment will pass over us.

Jesus is the Greater Light foreshadowed in the Fourth Day of Creation.

Jesus is the Fulfilment of the Law, meeting its requirements on our behalf and enabling us to live by its standard of love through the help of the Holy Spirit.

Jesus is the True Tabernacle of God with Man, opening a New Way through the torn veil of His body into the Truth and Life of the very Holy presence of God (Hebrews 10:19-20). He is the True Sacrifice on the Altar, Waters of Cleansing, Bread of Life, Lamp of Truth, Incense of Intercession and Mercy Seat.

Jesus is the True Perfect High Priest and All-Sufficient Sacrifice taking away our sins once and for all time.

Jesus is our True Sabbath Day Rest foreshadowed in the Seventh Day of Creation when He returns during the Millennium.

Jesus is the Fulfilment of the 7 Feasts of God - the True Passover Lamb who lived a sinless (unleavened) life, the Firstfruit among the elect, the Giver of the Holy Spirit on Pentecost, our Hope of redemption when He returns at the Last Trumpet, our Perfect High Priest and Sacrifice on the Day of Atonement, and our final and eternal Tabernacle.

Jesus is our true Eighth Day Sabbath giving us eternal rest in His presence.

Jesus is our True Hanukiah, giving light to the world at His conception.

Jesus is our True Sabbatical Year of Rest and Jubilee Year of Freedom from our debt of sin.

Jesus is the True Manna from Heaven and Water of Life from the Rock of our salvation during our wilderness journey here on earth.

Jesus is the True Red Heifer Sacrifice, sold for the price of a female slave and crucified outside the camp by Roman soldiers to cleanse us.

Jesus is the True Bronze Snake that was lifted up for our salvation.

Jesus is the True Prophet referred to by Moses, making Jesus our Prophet, Priest and King.

Jesus is the True Joshua who leads us into the Promised Land of eternal rest.

Jesus is our True Kinsman-Redeemer by becoming a man so that He can redeem us as a near kin or relative, paying the full price by dying on the Cross.

Jesus is the True Son of David who fulfills God's covenant with Israel's greatest king to establish David's throne forever.

Jesus is the One whom the Prophets speak of - the *Messiah* who will come as a Suffering Servant and King of Kings, the Righteous Branch that will remove sin in one day, the Root of Jesse, Immanuel ("God with us"), a Stumbling Stone to Israel and Judah but a Cornerstone of Zion, Wonderful Counselor, Mighty God, Eternal Father, Prince of Peace, Light to the Gentiles, Redeemer, Son of Man, Rock cut out not by human hands that struck the feet of iron and clay and became a Mountain over the whole earth, the Good Shepherd that would be smitten and rejected ... the list goes on and on and on.

34. Day 4: Jesus Christ – Mission
✝

WE saw the many ways in which the Old Testament Scriptures point us to Jesus Christ the Man, the Only One who matters. As we turn now to the Gospels, we are given 4 unique portraits of Jesus, each highlighting a particular Mission.

MARK (c. AD 55-60) - The first to be written and targeting Roman Gentile believers, Mark is a short, fast-paced, action and miracles-oriented account portraying **Jesus as the Suffering Servant and Son of God.** Although Mark highlights Jesus' divine authority as God's Son, it does not touch on His ancestry or family line because the Roman Gentile readers then are unlikely to appreciate what it means and why it is significant. You could say that Mark is written in a simple and engaging style to reach out to a wide audience of ordinary folks.

LUKE (c. AD 60-62) - Addressing the Greek Gentiles, Luke is a systematic account portraying **Jesus as the Perfect Saviour of the World and Son of Man**. In Luke, Jesus' ancestry is traced all the way back to Adam the first man. This is to show the intellectually-minded Greek readers that Jesus is not just sent to the Jews but to all mankind as their Saviour. If Mark reads like a news tabloid, then Luke is like a lengthy research paper systematically laying out the details of Jesus' life.

MATTHEW (c. AD 70-80) - Aimed at the Jews, Matthew is written to show that Jesus fulfils the Old Testament prophecies as **God's Promised *Messiah* and King, the Son of David**. Jesus' family line is traced to Abraham and David as further proof to the Jews that Jesus is who they are waiting for. Matthew is therefore like the Jewish edition of the Gospels.

JOHN (c. AD 85) - Meant for everyone, John is a deeply intimate, reflective and spiritual account of **Jesus as the Divine "I AM" - God Himself**. Jesus is revealed as the Word that was with God and is God. By the time John wrote this Gospel, at least 50 years had passed since Jesus' death and resurrection. As many believers by then would not have seen Jesus personally or even met the Apostles or others who had known Jesus in person, some began to question if Jesus could come as a man and yet be fully God. John wrote this Gospel partly to counter these false teachings that were emerging then.

*Each of the four had the face of a **human being**, and on the right side each had the face of a **lion**, and on the left the face of an **ox**; each also had the face of an **eagle*** - Ezekiel 1:10

*The first living creature was like a **lion**, the second was like an **ox**, the third had a face like a **man**, the fourth was like a flying **eagle*** - Revelations 4:7

Some scholars have noticed a correlation between the 4 faces of the cherubim found in the verses above and the 4 roles or missions of Jesus as seen in the 4 Gospels - the Ox represents

Jesus' Servanthood, the Man reflecting how Jesus is the Son of Man, the Lion symbolizing Jesus as the Lion of Judah and King of Kings, and the Eagle a depiction of Jesus as God Himself. Taken together, the 4 Gospels portray **Jesus as both God and Man, Saviour of Jews and Gentiles, and finally as both Servant and King**.

*But **when the set time [Kairos] had fully come**, God sent His Son ... to redeem those under the law, that we might receive adoption to sonship* - Galatians 4:4-5

Turning back to our perspective of the 7 Days of Creation (see diagram on next page), we see that Jesus is the Greater Light that caps the end of the Fourth Day of Creation. If you recall, the completion of the Temple in AM 3000 marks the beginning of the Fourth Day of Creation, with Israel now fully equipped to act as God's lesser light. But when the set time or *Kairos* had fully come, which is a thousand years later in AM 3992, God sent His Son Jesus to redeem His people by dying for us on the Cross.

Now, the Gospel did not simply end here with all of us living happily ever after. We are, after all, only at the end of the Fourth Day of Creation with 3 more days to go. Instead, Jesus speaks of the need for Him to depart in order to herald in the New Life in the Spirit and Body of Christ and that there will be opposition culminating in the rule of the Antichrist before He returns again to finally establish His Millennial Reign.

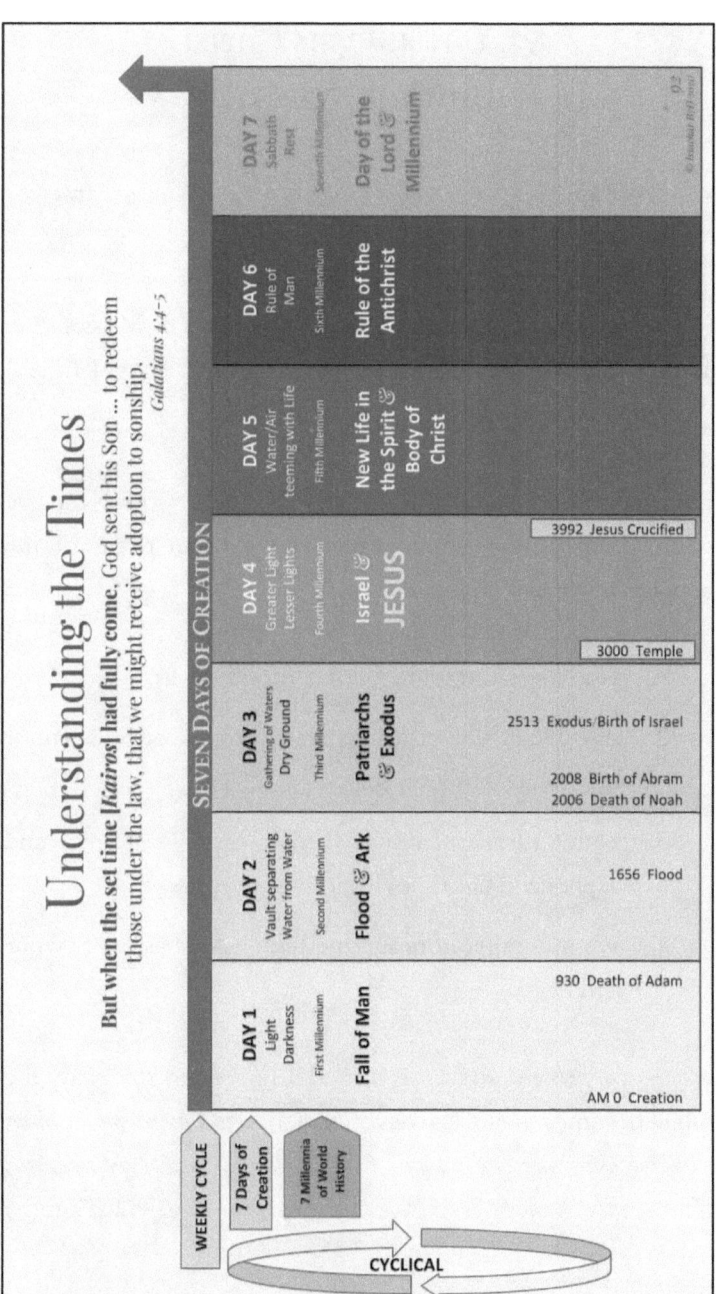

35. Day 4: Jesus Christ
- Unwhole Message

✝

"Believe in the Lord Jesus, and you will be saved - you and your household" - Acts 16:31

SO far, we have looked at Jesus the Man and His Mission. Let us now consider His Message, what Jesus actually taught and proclaimed during His brief time here on earth.

For many Christians, the Gospel of Jesus Christ can be summed up in the simple verse above or in terms of the popular 4 Spiritual Laws:

1. God loves us and has a plan for our lives;

2. But due to sin, we are separated from God and cannot experience His plan for us;

3. Only through Jesus Christ can we know and experience God's love and salvation; and

4. We must therefore receive Jesus Christ as our Saviour and Lord.

When we present the Gospel and Christianity this way, the Bible becomes mainly a devotional book, *"useful for teaching, rebuking, correcting and training in righteousness, so that the servant of God may be thoroughly equipped for every good work"* (2 Timothy

3:16-17). God's Word is reduced to a collection of stories, principles and sayings that teach moral values just like any other religious book, aside from the truth of this simplified Gospel.

While this approach is in itself not entirely wrong or inaccurate, it is dangerously unwhole or incomplete. This is because the Gospel message has been taken out of its wider Biblical context, a context that cannot be separated from its Jewish roots in Israel.

Unfortunately, our predominantly Gentile Church has built itself on the shallow foundation of this simplified Gospel and as a result, faces the danger of forgetting its Jewish origin and parentage. The Church cannot tell the difference between the Israel according to how God sees it as revealed to us in His Word, and the Israel and Judaism that rejected Jesus according to God's wisdom and plan. By rejecting and cutting Israel off completely and seeing itself now as the only and true lesser light of God, the Church misunderstands its own identity and misses its real purpose and destiny.

The truth is, Jesus Himself does not see the Gospel the way many of us view it. For Him, the Gospel is a continuation of a central narrative running through the entire Bible concerning God's Kingdom rule, first through Israel and now joined (and not replaced) by the Church.

This simplified Gospel may have been God's *Rhema* for His people the past 2,000 years. In God's wisdom, it may have indeed been sufficient for the Church during God's *Kairos* then to understand the Gospel in this simpler form for its task of evangelising the world. After all, it would have been difficult to understand the Gospel and the Church in relation to Israel, especially following Israel's disappearance as a nation after the Roman exile in AD 70.

But with Israel's rebirth in 1948 setting the stage for this final generation to witness the events that would befall Israel, the Church and the world leading up to Jesus' return, God's *Kairos* has come for us to hear His full *Rhema* and rediscover Jesus' message as He understands it.

36. Day 4: Jesus Christ – Unwelcome Message

✝

*The **time [Kairos] has come**,"* [Jesus] *said. "The **kingdom of God** has come near. Repent and believe the **good news**!"* - Mark 1:15

JESUS kicked off His earthly ministry with the above proclamation, which has great prophetic significance. In God's *Kairos* which was being fulfilled then at the end of the Fourth Day of Creation, Jesus came to His people Israel to bring the good news about the soon arrival of His Kingdom. We see here that the Gospel of Jesus Christ is not so much about us as it is about God and His Kingdom rule, beginning with Israel His chosen people and the Church the ingrafted branch of Israel. Our salvation is therefore not the end goal but the means, His lesser lights, through whom God will establish His Kingdom on earth in Jesus.

The Lord Himself will establish a house for you [David]: *When your days are over ... I will raise up your offspring to succeed you, your own flesh and blood ... and I will establish the throne of His* [the *Messiah's*] *kingdom forever* - 2 Samuel 7:11-13

In fact, the Jews in Jesus' day understood what Jesus meant perfectly. We saw earlier how the Old Testament Prophets had comforted God's people with the hope that a Promised *Messiah* would come to restore the glory of David's Kingdom to Israel.

The day when this *Kairos* event happens is known as the Day of the Lord. The Jews believe that on this special day, God will restore His rule over Israel to fulfill His promise to David mentioned in the verses above, even as Israel draws all nations to God as His lesser light.

"See, I will send the prophet Elijah to you before that great and dreadful day of the LORD comes" - Malachi 4:5

Now, although the Jews had returned to Jerusalem in 538 BC to rebuild the Holy City and God's Temple following their exile in Babylon, this promised kingdom never did come to pass. For the next 500 years, Israel was ruled and oppressed by a string of foreign powers - Medo-Persia, Greece and finally Rome in Jesus' time. In fact, the voice of the Prophets would go silent for over 400 years after the Prophet Malachi. In his closing words above however, Malachi reassured the people of God's faithfulness and prophesied that He would send a messenger, the Prophet Elijah, before the Day of the Lord came when the *Messiah* would appear.

Misplaced *expectations*

So, when John the Baptist suddenly came on the scene announcing that the *Messiah* was coming and later identifying Jesus to be the Anointed One, the Jews naturally had misplaced expectations that Jesus would rise up as a political leader to re-establish Israel as an independent kingdom. They remembered how a group of Jews had earlier led a revolt against the ruling Greek Seleucid Empire to establish what was known as the Hasmonean Dynasty. That kingdom lasted a century before being invaded by the Romans and replaced with the Herodian Dynasty just a generation earlier in 37 BC to act as Rome's puppet rulers.

Misplaced *values*

Other Jews, meanwhile, were more superficially drawn to the healings and various miracles that Jesus performed. Their misplaced values led them to seek the gifts rather than the Giver.

Misplaced *allegiance*

On the other hand, the Jewish political and religious leaders reacted in hostility and rejection toward Jesus. King Herod, who was actually only half Jew, feared for his own position and would not tolerate another "King of the Jews." The Sadducees, who were the elite of Jewish society then, did not want to see their comfortable lives shaken should the Romans come down hard on the Jewish nation for supporting this potential rebel King. Their misplaced allegiance to Rome revealed a heart that was far from God.

Misplaced *focus*

The Pharisees, meanwhile, hated Jesus for pointing out their hypocrisy. Theirs was a case of misplaced focus - they could not see the very God whom they claimed to worship because they majored in the minor, emphasizing slavish obedience to the smallest details of the Law but missing entirely God's spirit and heart behind these regulations.

For all the above reasons, Jesus' message would eventually be unwelcomed by the Jews. Let us not follow in their footsteps but instead ask God to correct our expectations, values, allegiance and focus, so that we truly understand Jesus' message for us in this *Kairos* moment.

37. Day 4: Jesus Christ - Unworldly Message

✝

*My kingdom is **not of this world*** - John 18:36

PREVIOUSLY, we saw how Jesus' message would eventually be unwelcomed by the Jews because of their misplaced expectations, values, allegiance and focus. It comes as no surprise then that when Jesus started describing the coming *Messianic* Kingdom, His message was unexpected, a far cry from what everyone, including John the Baptist and Jesus' own disciples, thought it would be.

They did not understand that the *Messiah* had to suffer first as the Lamb of God before returning in glory as the Lion of Judah; that His Kingdom was unworldly - not of this world or according to its standards or ways; nor were His Kingdom subjects to behave like those of this world. Instead, the people wanted to make Jesus King by force and so subject the Kingdom to the violent ways of this world (Acts 1:6, Matthew 11:2-6).

Because their eyes and ears were closed and their hearts hardened toward God, the people could not accept Jesus' Kingdom message. From then on, Jesus taught in parables so that *"Though seeing, they do not see; though hearing, they do not hear or understand"* (Matthew 13:13). The true nature of God's

Kingdom would remain a mystery or secret to the people and revealed only to Jesus' disciples.

Let us now go through the attributes of the *Messianic* Kingdom as taught by Jesus through His parables.

HIDDEN TREASURE, NARROW DOOR
Parables of the Hidden Treasure, Pearl

First, unlike earthly kingdoms that are visible to all, the Kingdom of God is like a hidden treasure that only a few will discover, a narrow door that not many will enter. One can only see it by faith and through the help of the Holy Spirit. One has to be called by God and born again in the spirit in order to hear Jesus our Good Shepherd's voice. But once we find God's Kingdom and realise its true value, we will gladly sacrifice and give up all we have to possess and enter it.

FIRST SHALL BE LAST, LAST SHALL BE FIRST
Parables of the Workers in the Vineyard, 2 Sons, Tenants, Wedding/Great Banquet

Next, although the nations of the world are also meant to benefit from God's covenant blessings for Abraham, Jesus had purposely reached out to only the Jews as they were God's chosen people. He already knew that they would reject His message and crucify Him as part of God's divine plan of salvation but nonetheless, they remained responsible for their choices and actions. Through these series of parables, Jesus delivers God's judgment on His existing Kingdom subjects - the lost sheep of Israel - for their unbelief and rejection, and in so doing opens the way for sinners, outcasts and Gentiles to enter into His Kingdom first before God turns His attention back to Israel again. In this way, the first (Israel) shall be last and the last (Gentiles) first.

LEAST IS THE GREATEST
Parables of the Lost Sheep, Lost Coin, Lost Son, Pharisee and Tax Collector

Again, contrary to the values of this world that define success in terms of results, accomplishments and numbers, Jesus emphasises the value of the least over the greatest, of the one over the many, and how the lowly and humble will be exalted in the Kingdom of God.

EXTRAORDINARY BUT MIXED GROWTH
Parables of the Growing Seed, Weeds, Mustard Seed, Yeast, Net, Bad and Good, Sheep and Goats

Moving on, Jesus devotes the most number of parables to explain that while the Kingdom of God will experience extraordinary growth, it will be a mixed group comprising those who belong to Him and those who don't. The extraordinary growth itself is something that is not only unnatural but ungodly, as seen in the Parables of the Mustard

Seed and Yeast - because mustard plants usually develop into bushes and do not grow into large trees, while yeast is associated with sin in the Bible.

All this however should come as no surprise. We had already seen how both Israel and the Church are imperfect vessels for God. Also, we just saw how God's ways are different from the ways of this world - what appears good to us may not be good to God, and what is not good can yet be good in God's hands.

LONG TIME IN COMING, SUDDEN RETURN

Lastly, we will consider later the end-time Bible passages where Jesus speaks of His return to bring to completion His Kingdom. What we want to highlight here are Jesus' words that it will be a long time in coming - again, contrary to our human expectations and impatient desire to have things happen according to our times and ways. But when it is time, His return will be sudden, at a day and hour that is unknown - again, when we least expect and are least prepared for Him.

38. Day 4: Jesus Christ
- Un"we" Message
†

GIVEN the unworldly nature of the Kingdom of God, Jesus teaches that those who follow Him will need to be:

RECEPTIVE
Parables of the Sower, Persistent Widow

Firstly, receptive in thought to His Word in order to be fruitful and a light for the Kingdom. We see this in the Parable of the Sower. Jesus also speaks of the need to have childlike faith, humility and persistence as seen in the Parable of the Persistent Widow.

REPENTANT
Sermon on the Mount, Parables of the Rich Fool, Rich Man and Lazarus, Shrewd Manager, Good Samaritan, Unmerciful Servant, Faithful Servant, Ten Virgins, Bags of Gold, Minas, Fig Tree

Next, repentant in deed, meaning to turn away from the world and follow Jesus, seeking first His Kingdom and righteousness. This involves handling wealth correctly, an important matter that Jesus stresses through the several parables (Rich Fool, Rich Man and Lazarus, Shrewd Manager). He also calls us to understand the very real cost of discipleship, which may include persecution.

It also means submitting to God's Kingdom rule and values in our lives as seen in Jesus' Sermon on the Mount and through various other Parables (Good Samaritan, Unmerciful Servant, Faithful Servant, Ten Virgins, Bags of Gold, Minas, Fig Tree). This can be summarised in terms of demonstrating love and forgiveness as well as being faithful and ready for His return.

REBORN

Lastly, reborn in spirit, to be born again in the Holy Spirit without which we cannot enter the Kingdom of God. Jesus promises that those who believe in Him will receive the Holy Spirit. Through the Spirit, God "circumcises" our hearts, cutting off the hardened and sinful parts in us so that we can be fruitful.

Coming back to our earlier discussion on the Gospel message, we see that the Good News of Jesus Christ is an un"we" message - not so much about our personal salvation and God's plan for our lives. It was, is, and will always be about Jesus and His Kingdom rule over all creation and eternity.

As we conclude these messages forming the bulk of our Lord's *Rhema*, may we hear, understand and obey what is being spoken to us today.

REFLECTIONS - Gospel of Jesus Christ

Jesus did many other things as well. If every one of them were written down, I suppose that even the whole world would not have room for the books that would be written - John 21:25

I wonder if the Apostle John was aware of how prophetic his above words would be when we consider the numerous books, sermons etc - both good and bad - that have been written about Jesus since John's Gospel. If we dare to be brutally honest about it, God's *Rhema* in the Bible and the Gospel of Jesus Christ is in danger of being drowned by all these human voices and noises, especially in this era of the information age and rise of fake news.

We see, hear and read more about God and His Word (Bible and Jesus) than we see God Himself, hear directly His *Rhema* voice and read from His Sacred Word. If you ask any genuine, God-seeking Christian out there, many will admit that they are lost and perplexed as to where to begin in their quest to know God in a more truthful and personal way.

But don't be dismayed. God is certainly aware of this situation and remains in full control. As Jesus told Nicodemus in John 3:8, the Holy Spirit moves as it pleases and we "*cannot tell where it comes from or where it is going.*" I am sure that much of what has been written, said or shown are truly driven by God's Spirit and for His glory, and even those that are not are permitted by God according to His will.

God has already warned us through the Creation Account that even as the Holy Spirit brings forth New Life characteristic of the Fifth Day of Creation, this will be quickly overtaken by the opposing spirit of the Antichrist characteristic of the Sixth Day that we are living in today. This unholy spirit manifests itself in the rule or kingdom of man that is opposed to God's Kingdom. It is also at work within the Church as we had seen in our brief survey of Church history earlier and will see in greater detail later on. We saw how Jesus warns us of this when He describes the Kingdom of God on earth as comprising both good and bad, true and counterfeit.

But how then should we proceed? How do we discern?

BACK TO BASICS

For the wisdom of this world is foolishness in God's sight
- 1 Corinthians 3:19

Simplicity of the Gospel (*vs* a simplistic Gospel)

The answer, as you might expect, can only be found in His Word. As we move on to study the New Testament Letters, let us re-discover through our examination of the early Church what it means to live the New Life in the Spirit and Body of Christ. Let us get back to the basics - to the simplicity of the Gospel preached by the Apostles, which we should not confuse with the simplistic Gospel mentioned at the start.

Knowing the God of the Word and being indwelt and led by His Spirit

Most of all, let us get back to the *"Word made flesh"* (John 1:14) - Jesus Himself. When we not only know the Word of God but the God of the Word, when we not only know of or about Jesus but have a personal and living relationship with Him, His Spirit lives in us. Through the Holy Spirit, Jesus the Greater Light illuminates our minds to His Truth and opens our ears to His *Rhema* voice. May we know that man's wisdom is foolishness to God and our many words are fruitless and futile. Only God's word never returns to Him empty but accomplishes His desire and purpose.

39. Day 5: New Life in the Spirit & Body of Christ

✝

*And God said, "Let the **water** teem with living creatures, and let **birds** fly above the earth across the vault of the **sky**." ... And there was evening, and there was morning - the fifth day* - Genesis 1:20-23

*I will ask the Father, and He will give you another advocate to help you and be with you forever - the Spirit of truth ... I will not leave you as orphans; **I will come to you*** - John 14:16-18

Holy Spirit is the *Spirit of Christ*

WE saw how no one can enter the Kingdom of God unless they are born again in the Spirit. On the night before He was to be crucified, Jesus prepared His disciples for His soon departure, promising them that He would not leave them as orphans but would send them *"another advocate ... the Spirit of truth."* Jesus reassured them that He would come to them because the Holy Spirit is none other than the Spirit of Christ Himself.

The Holy Spirit - from the Hebrew *Ruakh* (meaning breath, wind or spirit) and *Hakodesh* (meaning Holy) or the Greek *Pneuma* (which also means breath, wind or spirit) - is the Third Person of the Holy Trinity after God the Father and Jesus. The Holy Spirit is the very Breath or Spirit of God.

God is at work in history, in Jesus, and in us *through the Holy Spirit*

The Holy Spirit is not the result of Jesus' finished work on the Cross. He is mentioned in the Old Testament and is the Channel through whom God most often worked in history. In His Spirit, God initiates and accomplishes His will through men. In fact, we cannot please God apart from His Spirit working in us.

Jesus was conceived, baptised and ministered in the Holy Spirit. In Jesus, the Holy Spirit accomplished God's divine will where Israel had earlier failed.

And now, through Jesus, we receive the Holy Spirit and are born again into the New Life as promised by God in the Old Testament (Ezekiel 36:25-27). This New Life marks the start of the Fifth Day of Creation.

Descriptions of the Holy Spirit
- Living Waters, Wine, Oil, Wind, Breath, Fire, Dove

There is a reason for associating the Holy Spirit with the Fifth Day of Creation, which concerns new life in the water and sky.

Throughout the Bible, we see the Holy Spirit described in relation to these 2 elements - as living waters (here, we have the words baptism, cleansing and pouring out of the Spirit), wine (to contrast against the infilling of the Spirit), or oil (symbolic of the anointing of the Spirit), and as wind or breath (making up 40% of all Old Testament references to the Holy Spirit, being born again from above, the wind in Pentecost), tongues of fire or dove.

It is only on the Sixth Day of Creation that we speak about life on earth - the earthly rule of man, being literally formed from dust in contrast to the divine rule of the Spirit.

New Life in the *Spirit* of Christ
- *Baptism* and *infilling* of the Holy Spirit

As mentioned earlier, the Holy Spirit is the Spirit of Christ in us, through whom we are born again into the New Life. We receive the baptism of the Holy Spirit usually at the point of conversion when we are convicted of sin by the Holy Spirit, repent and receive Jesus as our personal Lord and Saviour.

Thereafter, as we grow in our spiritual walk with God, we continually experience the infilling of the Holy Spirit as He cleanses, transforms and empowers us for His work and will. The Holy Spirit is our Comforter, Helper and Counsellor who leads us into all Truth - teaching, bringing to remembrance Jesus' words and glorifying and testifying of Him; who intercedes for us; who adopts us into God's family - restoring our true identity; and who guards our salvation until the day of redemption.

New Life in the *Body* of Christ
- *Acts* of the Holy Spirit

But beyond being just individuals, we are also joined with the larger Body of Christ by the Holy Spirit, to be used by Him to bring the Body to maturity with the fullness of the Gentiles. I want to stress this very important point - our new life in Jesus' Spirit cannot be separated from our new life in His Body the Church, regardless of its imperfections, challenges and failures, especially as Christ's return draws nearer. We will see how the Holy Spirit is at work in the growth and development of the early Church when we turn next to study the Acts of the Apostles, also known as the Acts of the Holy Spirit.

40. Day 5: Acts of the Holy Spirit – From Jerusalem to Babylon

✝

IN the book of Acts, we see how the Holy Spirit grew the early Church as He empowered both the Apostles and ordinary believers, baptising them into the Body of Christ and equipping them for service, building up the Church to be a fitting dwelling place for God, bringing about unity, raising up leaders and commissioning and making competent those to be sent out.

The table on the next page is a simple timeline of the first 70 years of the Church, during which time the entire New Testament was written. From the timeline, we can identify 4 distinct periods:

JEWISH CHRISTIANITY
Jerusalem

Christianity actually began as a Jewish religion centered in Jerusalem. The first believers were Hellenistic or Greek-speaking Jews present in the Holy City for Pentecost who heard the Gospel in their own dialects. At that time, there was a wider shift in influence in Jewish society from Hebrew to Greek-speaking Jews. These Hellenistic Jews, who came from outside the Promised Land, were even more "Jewish" than

ACTS OF THE HOLY SPIRIT

Period	Key City/Events	Key Personalities	New Testament Books
Jewish Christianity (33-48 AD)	**Jerusalem** Pentecost (33 AD) - from Jerusalem to Judea, Samaria and beyond; shift in influence from Hebraic to Hellenistic Jews Antioch (43 AD) - believers first known as Christians	Peter Stephen martyred (35 AD) Philip, Barnabas Conversion of Paul (35 AD) Conversion of Cornelius (40 AD) James martyred (44 AD)	James (late 40s AD)
Missionary Age (48-58 AD)	**Antioch** Paul's 1st missionary journey (48-50 AD) Jerusalem Council (50 AD) - emergence of Gentile "Christians" distinct from *Messianic* Jews Paul's 2nd missionary journey (51-53 AD) Paul's 3rd missionary journey (54-58 AD)	Paul Barnabas, John Mark Silas, Timothy, Luke Apollos	Galatians (50 AD) 1 & 2 Thessalonians (52-53 AD) **Mark (55-60 AD)** 1 & 2 Corinthians (55-57 AD) Romans (58 AD)
Beginning of the Times of the Gentiles (58-70 AD)	**Rome** Paul's journey/imprisonment in Rome (58-62 AD) Paul's 4th missionary journey (62-67 AD) Destruction of Jerusalem (70 AD)	Paul martyred (67 AD) Peter Martyred (68 AD)	Ephesians, Philippians, Colossians, Philemon (60-62 AD) **Luke, Acts (60-62 AD)** 1 & 2 Timothy, Titus (65-67 AD) 1 & 2 Peter (64-68 AD) Hebrews (67 AD) Jude (68 AD)
End of the Apostolic Age (70-100 AD)	**Babylon (Rome)**	Death of John (100 AD)	**Matthew (70-80 AD)** **John (85 AD)** 1, 2 & 3 John (85-95 AD) Revelations (95 AD)

the native-born Jews in their insistence on Temple worship and keeping the Jewish customs. They were the ones who stoned Stephen, the first martyr or believer who was killed for Christ, for undermining traditional Judaism. The Apostle Paul was one of these Jews, born in what is today South-Central Turkey, who actively participated in Stephen's death and led the subsequent persecution of the Church. Even among believers, these Jews would later become the "Judaizers" that harassed the Gentile Christians, insisting that they be circumcised and become Jewish converts before they could be accepted into the Christian faith.

Looking back however, we see the Spirit clearly at work in the growth of the early Church. Had it not been for the persecution then, the Church would not have been scattered and forced to bring the Gospel throughout Judea, Samaria and beyond in response to Jesus' command in Acts 1:8. Even then, we see the Apostles initially staying put in Jerusalem, while Philip the Evangelist only went as far as Samaria - the Samaritans being half Jews - and to the Ethiopian eunuch, who was likely a Jewish convert. It took God's conversion of Paul - "*a Hebrew of Hebrews*" (Philippians 3:5) and therefore one most qualified to challenge the Judaizers - to fulfill Jesus' commandment for the Gospel to go beyond Israel and the Jews to those living throughout the known world then. Paul became God's Apostle to the Gentiles - His chief evangelist and theologian of this new and distinct Christian faith.

MISSIONARY AGE AND THE EMERGENCE OF GENTILE CHRISTIANITY
Antioch

The next major development is the emergence of Gentile Christianity originating from Antioch and culminating in the convening of the Jerusalem Council in AD 50. As Paul embarked on the first of his missionary journeys from this city to bring the Gospel across the Roman Empire, many Gentiles came into the faith. However, they would soon be harassed by the Judaizers mentioned earlier. The Jerusalem Council overruled these Judaizers and upheld the central Christian doctrine that we are all saved or justified by grace through faith in Christ alone and not through circumcision or following the laws of Moses as a Jewish convert. As a result, Christianity broke out of its Jewish shell to become a distinct faith that will one day transform the Jewish people and nation according to God's eternal plan and will. This truth - justification by faith in Christ alone - will also rescue the Church during the Protestant Reformation from spiritual bondage.

BEGINNING OF THE TIMES OF THE GENTILES
Rome

A final significant event that shaped Christianity is the destruction of Jerusalem and the Jewish Temple in AD 70 even as Christianity took root in the heart of the Roman Empire. This marked the end of Israel as a nation and the beginning of the "Times of the Gentiles." It set into motion God's timetable to bring in the summer harvest of the fullness of the Gentiles as the Spirit, through the Church, moves across the nations up to this day. But now that God has brought Israel back to life in 1948, we can expect the end of the summer harvest soon.

END OF THE APOSTOLIC AGE
Babylon (Rome)

What is left are the events that marked the closing years of this Age of the Apostles. It was a time of persecution under the Roman authorities, leading both Peter and John to refer to Rome figuratively as Babylon. Like its evil predecessor, the Roman Empire destroyed Jerusalem and exiled the Jews. This age is also characterised by the emergence of false doctrines such as Gnosticism, which denies that Christ really came as a human being and advocates instead salvation through the pursuit of Gnosis or "special knowledge." Centuries later, Martin Luther would equate the apostate Roman Catholic Church of his time to Babylon.

This concluding period gives us a taste of what it will be like in the end times as widespread tribulation and apostasy sweep over the world and the Church with the rise of the end-time Babylon/Rome and rule of the Antichrist seen in the book of Revelations.

41. Day 5: *Rhema* of the Holy Spirit
– Apostolic Message 1 (Faith)

✝

WE turn now to look at the *Rhema* of the Holy Spirit as He spoke through the Apostles, especially Paul.

In terms of God's unfolding *Rhema*, we saw earlier the message of the Old Testament Prophets as summarised in the diagram on the next page. These Prophets ultimately pointed us to the *Messiah* and His Kingdom rule.

In God's *Kairos*, Jesus came to partially fulfill this Old Testament promise. Coming as *Messiah* ben Joseph, the Lamb of God and Saviour of the World, Jesus revealed that His Kingdom was not of this world - it would be like a hidden treasure, a narrow door, where the last would be first and the least would be greatest. While the Kingdom would experience extraordinary growth, Jesus warned that it would comprise those who truly belonged to Him and those who didn't. The Kingdom would only be made perfect when Jesus returned on the Day of the Lord which, though a long time in coming, would suddenly appear at God's appointed time. Until then, believers were called to receive His Word, repent and be reborn in the Holy Spirit in order to enter this Kingdom. Jesus also prayed for his disciples to be united in His Spirit as one Body of Christ.

THE PROPHETIC MESSAGE

God's discipline and exile of His people
God's sovereignty over and judgment of His enemies
Day of the Lord
Even as God's judgment unfolded, there is comfort, hope and restoration
Central to these, prophecy of the *Messiah* and His Kingdom rule

THE *MESSIANIC* MESSAGE

Arrival of the *Messiah* as the Lamb of God
His Kingdom is not of this world
Need to receive, repent and be reborn in the Spirit to enter the Kingdom
Prayer for unity of the Body of Christ

THE APOSTOLIC MESSAGE

New life in the Spirit and Body of Christ
in Faith, Hope and Love

In the New Testament Letters, the Apostles built upon this progressive revelation of God's *Rhema* found in the Old Testament prophecies and Jesus' words. If we can summarise their Apostolic message, it is about **living in the Spirit and Body of Christ in Faith, Hope and Love until Jesus returns**.

FAITH in Christ

This is the foundation of our Christian faith. We saw earlier the demands made by the Judaizers on Gentile believers and how Christianity might have remained a Jewish faith that would live or die along with the nation of Israel. Against this, the New Testament writers - especially Paul in his letters to the Galatians, Romans and Ephesians - as well as the Jerusalem Council affirmed this simple yet central truth that we are saved by grace through faith in Christ alone.

This freed Christianity from the clutches of Judaism just in time before Israel was wiped out for the next 2,000 years. However, when Rome became a Christian Empire 2 centuries later in AD 312, the Church became more and more "*of this world*" as Church and State, religion and politics, got entangled. The Church started to exert power and political influence over believers and the State by imposing all sorts of unbiblical religious demands, until the Protestant Reformation liberated Christianity from these chains.

Today, this important truth of the Gospel continues to be attacked both from inside and outside the Church. In response, we need to remember that the Gospel of Christ is simple, sufficient and supreme.

Our Christian faith is simple - Let us not be caught up in endless futile intellectual arguments that take us away from the plain message of the Gospel, or go in pursuit of some special knowledge or revelation like the Gnostics of John's day. It is not the increase of "knowledge" but knowing Jesus through a personal and intimate encounter and relationship with Him that truly matters.

Our Christ is sufficient - Jesus has done all that is necessary for our salvation. There is nothing we can do that will make God value us more than He already does, and no sin that we can commit that will make Him love us less. Our identity and worth is found in being His child by faith alone. Jesus is also more than enough for every situation we face - wisdom for understanding and discernment, grace and strength during trials and temptations, and courage, peace and joy under persecution.

Our Christ is supreme - Jesus is ruler over all and therefore victorious in all our battles and deserving our wholehearted devotion.

42. Day 5: *Rhema* of the Holy Spirit - Apostolic Message 2 (Hope)

✝

IN our previous reading, we looked at the *Rhema* of the Holy Spirit as spoken through the Apostles, beginning with the foundation of our Christian faith - Faith in Christ alone. This forms the solid rock on which we stand. But we are to do more than just stand still ...

HOPE through the Spirit

We are to walk with God in Hope through the Spirit. Here, the Gospel is not only simple but is God's wisdom and power enabling us to lead holy lives with the Holy Spirit's help. The Spirit is *"Christ in you, the hope of glory"* (Colossians 1:27).

We saw earlier how Jesus promised His disciples and those who believed in Him that He would not leave them alone but would send another Helper and Comforter to be with them. Ever since the day of Pentecost, believers of every generation the past 2,000 years have been baptised and infilled with the Holy Spirit to empower them in their lifelong journey with God even as God sets them apart within the Body of Christ for His Kingdom work and purposes. The Holy Spirit will not rest until the Body of Christ reaches its full maturity with the fullness of the Gentiles to prepare for Jesus' return.

Paradox of faith *vs* works

Now, the simple message of salvation by grace through faith alone has led some to mistakenly believe that we are "free" to live as we wish since we are already saved no matter what we do. This was the case with the Corinthian Church in Paul's time and among Churches today that preach what we call the "hyper grace" gospel. Against this, James warns that faith without works is dead while Paul urges believers *"to work out your salvation with fear and trembling"* (Philippians 2:12) and not use our freedom in Christ to become slaves to the flesh and sin again.

At the other extreme, there are those who insist on the need to continue to follow the Law of Moses or to engage in some other forms of holy works or else risk losing our salvation. Paul makes clear that such fleshly efforts will ultimately fail, or else Christ would have died for nothing.

So what is it? Do we or do we not work out our faith?

The solution to this apparent paradox of faith vs works can be found in Paul's call for believers to walk in the Spirit so as not to gratify the desires of the flesh. It is true that faith without works is dead. But it is equally true that works without faith are bound to fail, because apart from the Spirit, we will not succeed. Paul summarises this best in the following verses:

Although I want to do good, evil is right there with me. For in my inner being I delight in God's law; but I see another law at work in me, waging war against the law of my mind and making me a prisoner of the law of sin at work within me. What a wretched man I am! Who will rescue me from this body that is subject to death? Thanks be to God, who delivers me through Jesus Christ our Lord! - Romans 7:21-25

REFLECTIONS - Walking in the Spirit

If we live by the Spirit, let us also walk by the Spirit - Galatians 5:25

Now, many of us will probably want to know how we are to walk in the Spirit and in so doing have a faith that really works.

Strive against our *flesh*
Saturate our *mind* with God's Word
Shalom (Rest) our *spirit* in His Spirit

If I could sum it up in one sentence, we have to continually strive against our flesh and turn away from the things of this world; saturate our mind with God's Word, which is the sword of the Spirit to tear down our mental strongholds; and allow our inner spirit man to *shalom* or rest in God's Spirit, learning to move according to His rhythm of grace and allowing the Holy Spirit to minister to our deepest needs. For me, this has meant learning to pray in tongues as a personal spiritual discipline.

100% God (Holy Spirit), *100%* man

His divine power *has given us everything we need for a godly life ...*
For this very reason, ***make every effort*** *... "* - 2 Peter 1:3-7

The truth is we are dependent on God to work in us through His Spirit, but we are still called to do our part. God supplies, but we must still labour as Peter puts it very aptly in the above verses. We can square this circle by heeding this simple rule of thumb - work as though everything depends on us, but rest and trust in God as everything ultimately depends on Him.

Refined through *trials* and *persecutions*

Finally, we are refined through trials and persecutions, for it is often only then that we experience how real and powerful the Holy Spirit is. When it comes to physical exercise, we have heard the phrase, "no pain, no gain." If we don't sweat it, we won't get it. It is the same with our inner spirit man. We only grow spiritually when the going gets tough, not when we are comfortable and complacent. James touches on this when he encouraged the early Jewish believers to boldly live out their faith despite persecution. Paul explains how true spirituality and godliness is measured not by spiritual gifts and talents but a life that displays God's power amidst suffering and weakness. Peter, addressing believers during the great persecution under Roman Emperor Nero, speaks of how suffering is a part of God's will to purify our faith for His glory.

43. Day 5: *Rhema* of the Holy Spirit - Apostolic Message 3 (Love)

✝

*"**A new command** I give you: **Love one another.** As I have loved you, so **you must love one another.** By this everyone will know that you are My disciples, **if you love one another**"* - John 13:34-35

LOVE for the Body

WE saw how we are to stand in Faith in what Christ has done for us, and to walk in Hope through the transforming power of the Holy Spirit. But more than that, we are to walk with God in Love for the Body of Christ.

Jesus repeatedly stresses the heart or spirit of the Law - Love. This is why He rebuked the religious leaders in His time for their hypocrisy in following the letter but not the spirit of the Law. This is also why Jesus died for our sins - out of love for us.

Now, in His last words to His disciples before His arrest and crucifixion (John 13-17), Jesus called on them to remain in Him in love and obedience, giving them a new commandment as seen in the above verses. Jesus then prayed for unity not just among the disciples then but for all who would hear and believe in Him in the generations to come.

Bond of love *uniting* all believers

This bond of love uniting all believers is a key teaching of the Apostles. In his letter to the Galatians, Paul speaks of the unity of all believers in Christ and how they should use their freedom in Christ not to continue sinning but to serve one another in love. He rebuked the Corinthians for the quarrels and divisions within the church concerning matters that required love and unity, dismayed that they were only "united" when it came to tolerating sin.

Body of Christ
- *One* body but *many* parts, roles and functions

Just as a body, though one, has many parts, but all its many parts form one body, so it is with Christ. For we were all baptized by one Spirit so as to form one body - whether Jews or Gentiles, slave or free - and we were all given the one Spirit to drink - 1 Corinthians 12:12-13

Instead, speaking the truth in love, we will grow to become in every respect the mature body of Him who is the head, that is, Christ. From Him the whole body, joined and held together by every supporting ligament, grows and builds itself up in love, as each part does its work
- Ephesians 4:15-16

It was Paul who coined the term "Body of Christ" to describe this unity bringing together Jew and Gentile, male and female, slave and free. We are all equally children of God although each of us may have different spiritual giftings and callings, just as a human body has many different parts, each with its own role and function. God's purpose is so that, by serving one another in love and humility, the Body "*may be built up ... and become mature, attaining to the whole measure of the fullness of Christ*" (Ephesians 4:12-13).

REFLECTIONS - Love and Unity

State of the (*dis*)union

However, the Church's record on this has been far from perfect. Like Israel, the history of the Church has been marked by divisions and internal conflicts and all sorts of other weaknesses and failings from the very beginning. The Protestant Reformation, while restoring key biblical truths to the Body of Christ, created 40 major denominations and over 40,000 independent churches worldwide. We are far from the love and unity that Jesus commanded and prayed for.

Does this mean that God's purpose for the Church has failed? By no means! What appears to be a failure in our eyes is precisely God's way to bring about His miraculous plan, just as Israel's apparent failure and rejection of Jesus was according to the very will and mystery of God in Christ. We saw this happening to the early Church where, through developments that were entirely unplanned, the Gospel was brought to Judea, Samaria and beyond. The same can be said of the Church the past 2,000 years as it brings the Gospel throughout the world. God's ways are never our ways.

With this in mind, let us persevere in obeying Christ's command to love His Body, while resting in Him that the Holy Spirit will rule over the Church. Let us stop acting like the Corinthians, who took pride in arguing among themselves about useless spiritual-sounding topics but behaving as one when it came to matters of the flesh. In particular, let us look beyond our own local church or denomination to embrace God's people everywhere. I believe that as the Church enters into the Tribulation in the end times, this will be the "finest hour" for the Body of Christ - united not by our human plans or organisation but by the Spirit to walk the way of persecution and the Cross.

Charismatic **controversy**

One major obstacle to greater Church unity today is the divide between the charismatic and non-charismatic churches, between churches that believe in tongues, visions, prophecies, healings and other supernatural works of the Holy Spirit, and those that don't. Charismatics point to the "dead" faith of the non-charismatic churches and argue that they had abandoned the Spirit behind the Word of God. Non-charismatics, meanwhile, point to the false teachings and practices common among charismatic churches and accuse them of abandoning the Word to offer profane fire of the so-called "Spirit."

By pointing only to the extremes, each side risks throwing away what is of God along with what is not. The reality is that the Spirit and Word are one, just as Jesus and the Word are one. The Spirit speaks to us mainly through the Word and the Word can only be understood and bring forth fruit in our lives through the Spirit. The key therefore is not to reject the things of the Spirit but to *"test the spirits to see whether they are from God"* (1 John 4:1), and not to worship the spiritual gifts themselves but understand that these are given to serve the higher purpose of building up the Body of Christ, just as the Spirit is given not to draw attention to Himself but to give glory to Christ (John 16:13-15).

Israel *vs* Church

Ultimately, the love and unity of the Body must bring back together Israel and the Church. The union of Jews and Gentiles as one Body of Christ was the single most important issue in the closing days of Israel and the birth of the Church. If I could use an analogy from farming, the seed of the Gospel first sprouted among the Jews 2,000 years ago. However, it would not have made it past the nursery of Israel - which would soon be trampled by the Romans in AD 70 - to bring about the current worldwide harvest of souls had it not been for those Jewish believers then who overcame their own racial and religious prejudices to recognise how God was moving beyond their people and nation.

Today, this bringing together of Gentiles and Jews is again the single most important issue in the closing days of the Church and the rebirth of Israel as God's Millennial Kingdom. We know that the harvest is quickly coming to an end with the fullness of the Gentiles. However, it will not be gathered out of the fields of the Church - which will soon be trampled by the Antichrist - and be brought back into the storehouse of Israel to await the return of our King until we overcome our own spiritual prejudices to recognise the hand of God beyond what we know as the Body of Christ.

Some commentators believe that the Church will be raptured first, leaving behind Israel and the wicked world to suffer during the Tribulation. This perspective goes against the bulk of what the Bible teaches us and, more importantly, the very nature of God. It denies the unity of Jews and Gentiles, and the prophetic bond between Israel and the Church that points more to the rupture and earthly exile rather than the rapture and spiritual homecoming of the Church (we will talk more about this later). It holds a flawed one-sided view of God and plays down His divine, good and perfect purposes in refining His people through the suffering and persecution that is characteristic of the way of the Cross.

44. Day 6: Rule of the Antichrist

✝

*God said, "**Let Us make mankind** in Our image, in Our likeness, **so that they may rule** ... God saw all that He had made, and it was **very good**. And there was evening, and there was morning - the sixth day* - Genesis 1:24-31

GOD created Man on the Sixth Day to rule over Creation. Man, having been formed in God's image, was to be His caretaker over the earth as an act of service and worship. However, what was originally intended to be *"very good"* became very bad with the Fall of Man.

Kingdom of man (*vs* Kingdom of God)

Previously, we mentioned the emergence of a Satan-inspired kingdom or rule of man beginning with the Tower of Babel. We later saw how this kingdom, in the form of the ancient empires of Babylon and Rome, destroyed God's Holy City Jerusalem and exiled His people twice.

In the end times, Satan will raise up an evil world power - a revived Roman-Babylonian empire - to destroy Israel. He will also seduce the Church, luring her away from God to run after the things of this world. This apostate Church - "Babylon the Prostitute" as revealed to John in Revelations - will turn against the faithful of God in the Body of Christ. This kingdom of man that opposes God's Kingdom throughout history was what was revealed to Nebuchadnezzar in Daniel 2.

Spirit of the Antichrist (*vs* Spirit of Christ) in the kingdom of man

It is a demonic kingdom working under the spirit of the Antichrist, just as God's Kingdom is directed by the Holy Spirit, the Spirit of Christ.

We see the spirit of the Antichrist at work:

In the first son of man, Cain, when he murdered his brother. Just as Cain was jealous that God favoured Abel's offering, Satan the Angel of Light is jealous that God favours Man to be His lesser light, God having made us in His image to reflect His divine light and glory.

In Nimrod, whose name means "Rebel," who established the first kingdom of man in Babylon where the Tower of Babel was later built.

In Pharaoh, the hardened heart who tried to destroy God's chosen people, Israel, when they were in Egypt.

In Nebuchadnezzar, who destroyed the First Temple and exiled the Jews to Babylon.

In Herod, who tried to kill the infant Jesus.

Spirit of the Antichrist in the Kingdom of God

And in Israel, God's very chosen nation, whose leaders crucified the *Messiah*.

Even within the Body of Christ, we see how throughout Church history the divine life brought about by the Holy Spirit characteristic of the Fifth Day of Creation is quickly robbed away by the opposing spirit of the Antichrist characteristic of the Sixth Day of Creation.

This unholy spirit was already at work among the Apostles. Had it not been for the overwhelming power of the Holy Spirit that came upon them during Pentecost, the natural inclination of the Apostles was to fight amongst themselves for position and power within Christ's Kingdom.

As the hope for Christ's soon return faded over time and with Christianity becoming the official religion of the Roman Empire, the Church became more and more of this world. What the Apostles had earlier struggled against - earthly power and politics - became the focus and ambition of the Church as man started to justify their own rule in the name of God.

This rule of man within the Kingdom of God culminated in the Great Schism or division in AD 1054 (AM 5013) - marking the beginning of the Sixth Day of Creation - when the Bishop or Pope of Rome declared himself head over all the other key bishops with authority over the entire universal Church.

"No king can reign rightly unless he devoutly serves Christ's Vicar ...
The priesthood is the Sun, the kingdom the Moon"
- Pope Innocent III (AD 1198-1216)

Indeed, Pope Innocent III put forward the famous idea above that the Emperor was the moon or lesser light to the Pope's sun or greater light, meaning that the Pope ruled not only over the Church but over all the earth's kingdoms and nations.

The Kingdom of God has now become the kingdom of this world!

RULE OF THE ANTICHRIST (*vs* Rule of Christ)
- Joining together of *State* (Roman-Babylonian Empire) and *Church* (Babylon the Prostitute)

As we approach the end of the Sixth Day of Creation in our generation, we can expect the unholy spirit of the Antichrist that has been working in the kingdoms of man and God to come together to form the rule of the Antichrist, the end-time Roman-Babylonian Empire and Babylon the Prostitute that we mentioned earlier.

This "Age of Empires" joining together the State and Church has happened before, beginning with the Christian Roman Empire which lasted from the time of Emperor Constantine in AD 312 to AD 476 in the West, and AD 1453 in the East (known as the Byzantine Empire).

Following the fall of Rome, there were efforts to revive the Western Roman Empire as the Holy Roman Empire by both the French and Germans, with the Holy Roman Emperors crowned by the Roman Popes of that time.

This was followed by Napoleon Bonaparte (AD 1804-1814) and ultimately Adolf Hitler (AD 1933-1945).

In Hitler's Third Reich or "Third Empire" which he declared would last a thousand years like Christ's Millennium, the Jewish Holocaust where 6 million Jews were slaughtered on this Sixth Day of Creation (incidentally, there are about 6 million Jews in Israel today), and the German Church during that period comprising the apostate Nazi national church and the true "confessing church," we are given the clearest glimpse yet into how the future kingdom of the Antichrist may look like.

Finally, we need to consider the role that Islam and the Muslim countries could play in this end-time demonic kingdom. Islam is the dominant religion in those areas occupied by Israel's former enemies. It is on the rise in Europe. Finally, there are attempts to bring Christianity and Islam together as one religion for the sake of peace.

When we fit all these pieces together, we see the beginnings of the end-time evil empire of the Antichrist.

45. Day 6: Living in the Last Days
✝

LET us now look at the key events from the time of Jesus' departure and the birth of the Church until His soon return on the Day of the Lord (see diagram on the next page).

Last days, *literally*

It is not wrong to say that we have been living in the "last days" since the time of Christ, as the past 2,000 years are literally 2 days - the Fifth and Sixth Days of Creation - before Jesus returns to usher in the Seventh or Sabbath Day rest of His Millennial rule according to what the Creation Account tells us.

So what should we expect in these last days?

Beginning of birth pains and first 4 seals of Revelation 6

First, Jesus tells us that there will be deception, war, famine, natural calamities and plagues, but that these are only the "*beginning of birth pains*" (Matthew 24:8). These signs correspond to the opening of the first 4 seals mentioned in Revelations 6. When we take these signs together with the fifth seal concerning the persecution of the saints, we see that they are what the Old Testament Prophets have foretold as God's way of disciplining His people and judging His enemies.

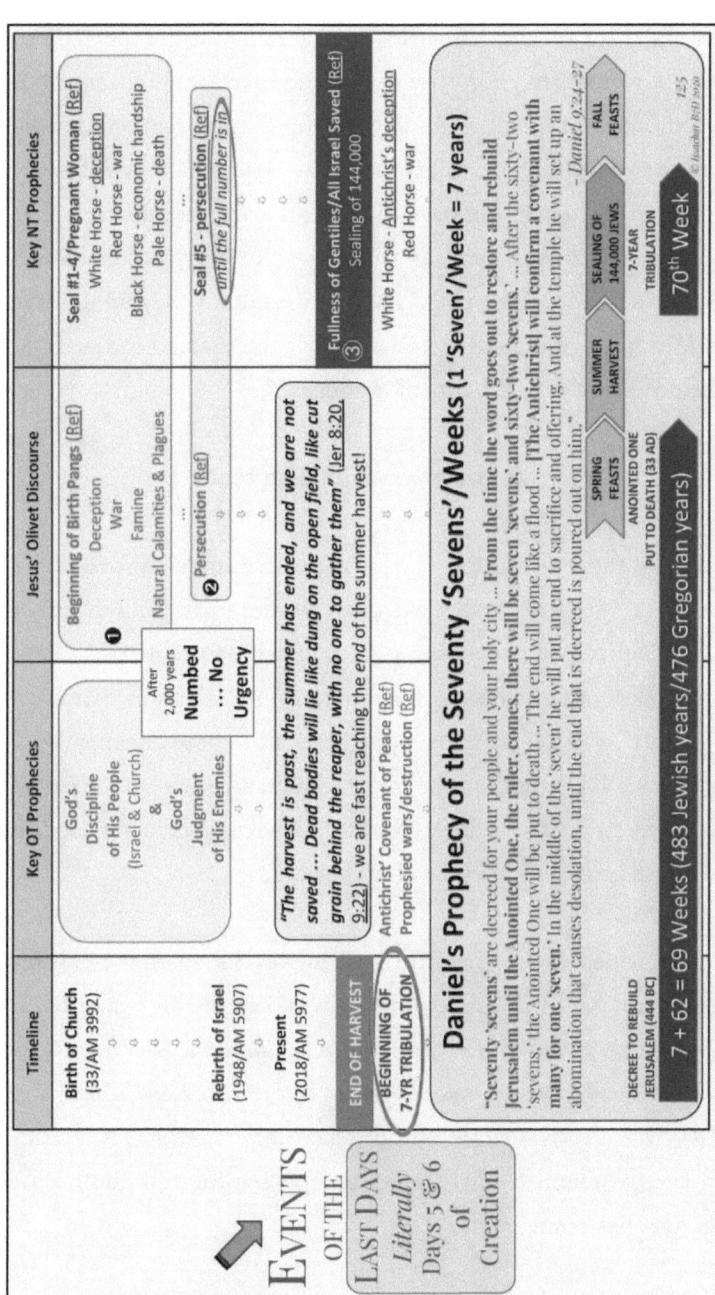

As the Day of the Lord draws nearer, we can expect these events to happen more frequently and increase in severity but we should not be alarmed, as such things must happen but the end is still to come. Unfortunately, many had prematurely sounded the alarm the past 2,000 years so Christians today are numbed to its urgency at this *Kairos* moment when God's *Rhema* is finally telling us NOW that the end of the end times is indeed here! May we see and correctly understand the signs of the times as they are happening today.

Persecution - The fifth seal

Second, the persecution of the saints mentioned above is the other key feature of the last days. As the early Church writer Tertullian puts it, "*the blood of the martyrs is the seed of the Church.*" Jesus alerts us to this on many occasions. Salvation may be a free gift of grace by faith, but it does not come cheap. Christ paid with His blood on the Cross and many of us will be called to do likewise. How different this Gospel sounds compared to what we hear among some churches today!

At the opening of the fifth seal in Revelations 6:9-11, John heard the cries for justice of those who had died for their faith. They were given white robes and told "*to wait a little longer, until the full number of their fellow servants, their brothers and sisters, were killed just as they had been.*" God is keeping count and is faithful to avenge them in His perfect time, when the full number of martyrs has come in.

Fullness of the Gentiles and start of the Tribulation

"The harvest is past, the summer has ended, and we are not saved ... Dead bodies will lie like dung on the open field, like cut grain behind the reaper, with no one to gather them" - Jeremiah 8:20, 9:22

Third, the fullness of the Gentiles. This is different from the full number of those who have died for their faith. We have already discussed before what this term means. What I want to highlight here is that the fullness of the Gentiles, once reached, not only marks the end of the summer harvest, the Age of Grace or Church Age, but also signals the start of the 7-year Tribulation.

Let me briefly explain. In a prophecy given to Daniel, we are told that the full cycle of God's sacred time is made up of 70 'sevens' or weeks (here, one 'seven' or week refers to 7 years). This is made up of 69 weeks from the time of Cyrus' decree to rebuild Jerusalem in 444 BC until the time of Christ's crucifixion in AD 33, and a final 70th week - the 7-year Tribulation.

When we match this timetable against the 7 Feasts of God, we see that the first 69 weeks ended with the Spring Feasts marking Jesus' coming and birth of the Church, while the 70th week will end with the Fall Feasts when Jesus returns. For the past 2,000 years therefore, we have been living in that summer interval between the 69th and 70th week of Daniel's prophecy.

But once the fullness of the Gentiles is reached, the world harvest will end as God turns His attention back to Israel with the sealing of those Jews who belong to Him and to the final Tribulation events that will take place before Jesus returns. There will be no more Gentile harvest from this point on as described so vividly by Jeremiah in the above verses.

Rupture *vs* rapture

We saw how Satan will seduce the Church into prostituting herself to the world and how the State and Church will therefore come together under the rule of the Antichrist in the end times. Instead of a rapturous return to Christ, the Church will experience a rupturing of an unimaginable scale, resulting in widespread persecution of the saints of God until the full number of those who are to die for their faith is in.

Revelations speak of "*a great multitude that no one could count, from every nation, tribe, people and language ... who have come out of the great tribulation* [through martyrdom]," of how the Dragon (Satan) would wage war against "*those who keep God's commands and hold fast their testimony about Jesus*," how the Beast (Antichrist) "*was given power to wage war against God's holy people and to conquer them*," how Babylon the Prostitute (Apostate Church) "*was drunk with the blood of God's holy people, the blood of those who bore testimony to Jesus*," and therefore how "*this calls for patient endurance and faithfulness on the part of God's people ...* [for] *Blessed are the dead who die in the Lord from now on*" (Revelations 7:9-14, 12:17, 13:7, 17:5-6, 14:12-13).

46. Day 6: Tribulation Week
✝

PREVIOUSLY, we looked at the last days which, seen from the perspective of the 7 Days of Creation, refer to the past 2,000 years since the time of Christ and birth of the Church. We saw how Jesus warns us that there will be deception, war, famine, and natural calamities and plagues, but that these are only "*the beginning of birth pains*," how believers will be persecuted until the full number of those who are to die for their faith is in, and finally how the fullness of the Gentiles, once reached, marks the end of the summer harvest, the Age of Grace or Church Age, and the beginning of the 7-year Tribulation. There will be no more Gentile harvest from this point on as the Church experiences its greatest ever earthly rupture rather than a heavenly rapture. In such a time, we are called to patiently endure and remain faithful as we enter into this final stretch of history before Jesus returns.

As we turn now to the Tribulation Week itself, there are 4 key events or things to take note of (see diagram on the next page).

A *false* peace

First, the Antichrist will "*confirm a covenant with many for one 'seven'*" (Daniel 9:26-27). This will likely occur on the Feast of Trumpets, which is also the Jewish New Year, to mark the start of a New Year or new beginning for Israel and the world.

EVENTS OF THE LAST DAYS
Literally Days 5 & 6 of Creation

Timeline	Key OT Prophecies	Jesus' Olivet Discourse	Key NT Prophecies
Birth of Church (33/AM 3992) ◊ ◊ ◊ **Rebirth of Israel** (1948/AM 5907) ◊ **Present** (2018/AM 5977) ◊	God's Discipline of His People (Israel & Church) & God's Judgment of His Enemies	**① Beginning of Birth Pangs** (Ref) — Deception — War — Famine — Natural Calamities & Plagues ◊ **② Persecution** (Ref) ◊	**Seal #1-4/Pregnant Woman** (Ref) — White Horse - deception — Red Horse - war — Black Horse - economic hardship — Pale Horse - death ◊ **Seal #5 - persecution** (Ref) *until the full number is in* ◊
END OF HARVEST			**Fullness of Gentiles/All Israel Saved** (Ref) Sealing of 144,000 ③
BEGINNING OF 7-YR TRIBULATION ◊ **MID-WEEK/ BEGINNING OF GREAT TRIBULATION** ◊ ◊ ◊ ◊ **END OF TRIBULATION**	④ Antichrist' Covenant of Peace (Ref) Prophesied wars/destruction (Ref) ⑤ Abomination of Desolation (Ref) *for 3½ years* ◊ ◊ ◊ ⑦ Cosmic Signs (Ref)	**TIME OF JACOB'S TROUBLE** (Jer 30:7) Abomination of Desolation & Jerusalem Trampled (Ref) *until end of Times of Gentiles* ⑥ Gospel Preached (Ref) Cosmic Signs (Ref)	White Horse - Antichrist's deception Red Horse - war **Abomination of Desolation & Jerusalem Trampled (Two Witnesses)** *by Gentiles for 42 months/1260 days* (Ref) **Gospel Preached** (Ref) *by supernatural means* **Seal #6 - Cosmic Signs** (Ref) **Seal #7 - Outpouring of God's Wrath** 7 Trumpets & 7 Bowls judgment (Ref)

"The harvest is past, the summer has ended, and we are not saved ... Dead bodies will lie like dung on the open field, like cut grain behind the reaper, with no one to gather them" (Jer 8:20, 9:22) - we are fast reaching the end of the summer harvest!

DAY OF THE LORD

This will also kick off the Tribulation countdown and the start of what is known as the "*time of Jacob's trouble*" (Jeremiah 30:7), a time of great fear and trembling for Israel as God uses this period to wrestle His chosen nation into submission like the way He did with Jacob (Genesis 32:22-32).

This covenant or treaty is likely a deceptive offer of world peace, as the Antichrist promises through his demonic kingdom to put an end to the Israeli- Palestinian/Arab conflict and also the wider "clash of civilisations" between Christianity and Islam. Israel will, for the first time since its rebirth in 1948, be "*a land of unwalled villages ... a peaceful and unsuspecting people*" (Ezekiel 38:11). The third Jewish Temple will also be built then, likely side-by-side with the Dome of the Rock/Al-Aqsa Mosque and perhaps even a Church as the Temple Mount becomes the prime example of world peace and inter-faith harmony.

Ironically though, in this new age of "peace" and "enlightened tolerance," we will witness an increasing intolerance of those who refuse to compromise their faith, something that is already happening today. There will arise widespread suppression of true believers by governments and even by their own churches as the world buys into this deceptive argument. The path to world peace will be paved with the bodies of possibly millions of God's faithful, their cries drowned by the shouts of those celebrating this new world order under the Antichrist and his False Prophet.

However, this false peace will not last. The Old Testament prophecies record at least 2 major wars that have yet to be fulfilled. The deception, war, famine, natural disasters and persecution mentioned earlier will continue until the very end.

Abomination of desolation

Second, after 3½ years (that is, midway through the Tribulation Week on the Feast of Passover of the fourth year), the Antichrist will break this covenant to set up what is known as the "*abomination of desolation*" (Daniel 9:27b, Matthew 24:15) in the Temple. He will declare himself the Passover Lamb, defiling the Temple by making himself God and Christ. Aided by the False Prophet and 10 leaders who will come into power then, the Antichrist will trample Jerusalem, blaspheming God and persecuting God's people while deceiving the rest of the world and making them receive the mark of the Beast (666). He will also destroy his former ally, the Apostate Church, and go to war with various nations.

Great Tribulation

The remaining half of this 7-year period is known as the Great Tribulation. Jesus describes how "*Jerusalem will be trampled on by the Gentiles until the times of the Gentiles are fulfilled*" (Luke 21:24b), while John describes in detail in Revelations the key events and characters during this period. In particular, John speaks of the miraculous display of God's power and judgment by the Two

Witnesses (Revelations 11:1-12) - possibly Moses and Elijah, both having performed such amazing acts in their lifetimes and who were with Jesus at His Transfiguration. There will be a spike in all the calamities unleashed by the first 5 seals as well as in demonic activity, as Satan will have been thrown down to earth during this period and knows that his time is short.

Great Commission

Third, now those who believe that we can "speed up" Christ's return by finishing the task of world evangelisation often quote Jesus' words in Matthew 24:14 that *"this gospel of the kingdom will be preached in the whole world as a testimony to all nations, and then the end will come."* While we should certainly try our best to fulfill the Great Commission, when we realise that just prior to this (see Matthew 24:9-13) Jesus speaks of persecution, of many turning away from the faith and betraying and hating each other, of many false prophets appearing and deceiving many people, and of increasing wickedness, where the love of most will grow cold and one needs to fight to even stand firm in the faith just to be saved, let alone save others, it is clear that Jesus is not referring to a victorious Church winning over the world. If anything, it will be despite the Church.

As John later reveals in Revelations 14:6-7, the Gospel will be preached by divine means, likely through the supernatural witnessing of the Two Witnesses as we will see later. The purpose here is not to evangelize the world, to bring about salvation, for the fullness of Gentiles will have already come in by then. Rather, it is to announce that "*the hour of His judgment has come*," for the wicked will remain unrepentant and defiant towards God even after being confronted with the Gospel.

Cosmic signs and outpouring of God's wrath

Finally, the Great Tribulation climaxes with a series of cosmic signs and the outpouring of God's wrath on the wicked with the breaking of the last 2 seals and releasing of the 7 trumpets and bowls judgments described in Revelations. The Old Testament Prophets also speak of great cosmic signs that will mark the Day of the Lord, while Jesus describes how these signs will accompany His return. Now, given how similar the 7 trumpets and bowls judgments are to the miracles performed by the Two Witnesses, it is likely that these judgments are the means through which the Two Witnesses demonstrate the truth and power of the Gospel before a wicked and unrepentant world.

As we conclude, let us bear in mind that there are 3 conditions, all known only to God, that must be fulfilled before Christ returns:

Fullness of the Persecuted
Fullness of the Gentiles
Fullness of the Gospel

Only then will the end come with the Day of the Lord.

47. Day 7: Day of the Lord
✝

*Thus the heavens and the earth were completed in all their vast array. By the **seventh** day God had finished the work He had been doing; so on the **seventh** day He rested from all His work. Then God blessed the **seventh** day and made it holy, because on it He rested from all the work of creating that He had done* - Genesis 2:1-3

THE Day of the Lord marks the beginning or sundown as it were of the Seventh and Final Day of Creation, before giving way to the glorious dawn or sunrise of the New Millennium of Christ's rule (remember, the Jewish day starts at sunset). It is the end of the world as we know it, a dreadful day where God's discipline of His people and judgment of His enemies reach their climax. As Israel and the world plunges into the dark and fearsome night of the rule of the Antichrist during the Tribulation period, God will pour out His wrath upon the wicked and unrepentant through His Two Witnesses.

Nations gather *against* Jerusalem and Israel

As recorded in various Old and New Testament passages, all these will culminate in Satan's last-ditch attempt to destroy God's people by gathering the nations against Jerusalem and Israel, even as the Antichrist overpowers and kills the Two Witnesses to the delight of the wicked. At this eleventh hour just days before the nation is to celebrate the Fall Feasts, Israel finally acknowledges and cries out in desperation and true repentance for her *Messiah*.

At that moment, the Two Witnesses come back to life, striking terror in the hearts of the wicked. They then ascend to heaven as a great earthquake strikes Jerusalem, destroying a tenth of the Holy City and killing 7,000 inhabitants. The Mount of Olives is split from East to West, and Jerusalem is raised up high with a fountain of water opening up from under the Temple.

There will be great cosmic signs - "*the sun will be darkened, and the moon will not give its light; the stars will fall from the sky, and the heavenly bodies will be shaken ... on the earth, nations will be in anguish and perplexity at the roaring and tossing of the sea. People will faint from terror, apprehensive of what is coming on the world.*" "*Then the kings of the earth, the princes, the generals, the rich, the mighty, and everyone else, both slave and free, hid in caves and among the rocks of the mountains. They called to the mountains and the rocks, 'Fall on us and hide us from the face of Him who sits on the throne and from the wrath of the Lamb! For the great day of Their wrath has come, and who can withstand it?'*" (Joel 3, Ezekiel 38-39, 47, Zechariah 12-14, Matthew 23:39, 24:29, Luke 21:25, Revelations 6:15-17, 11:7-13).

At midnight *the cry rang out: 'Here's the bridegroom! Come out to meet him!'* - Matthew 25:6

Then, at midnight as it were, on the Feast of Trumpets, "*The seventh angel sounded his trumpet, and there were loud voices in heaven, which said: 'The kingdom of the world has become the kingdom of our Lord and of His Messiah, and He will reign for ever and ever.*"

"Then will appear the sign of the Son of Man in heaven. And then all the peoples of the earth will mourn when they see the Son of Man coming on the clouds of heaven, with power and great glory. And He will send His angels with a loud trumpet call, and they will gather His elect from the four winds, from one end of the heavens to the other."

At that very moment, *"in a flash, in the twinkling of an eye, at the last trumpet … the dead will be raised imperishable, and we will be changed … For the Lord Himself will come down from heaven, with a loud command, with the voice of the archangel and with the trumpet call of God, and the dead in Christ will rise first. After that, we who are still alive and are left will be caught up together with them in the clouds to meet the Lord in the air."*

(Matthew 24:30-33, Mark 13:26-29, Luke 21:27-31, 1 Corinthians 15:51-52, 1 Thessalonians 4:15-18, Revelations 11:15).

Wedding supper of the Lamb
Great supper of God

Because of the great cosmic disturbances during this time, it is plausible that the 10 days between the Feast of Trumpets (1 Tishri) summoning God's people to meet the Lord in the air, and the Day of Atonement (10 Tishri) when Jesus returns and sets foot on the Mount of Olives to rescue and restore a repentant Israel while judging the nations, are compressed into a single day so that these two events happen at the same time.

If this is so, then the Wedding Supper of redemption and restoration of God's people with Jesus the Lamb is also the Great Supper of judgment of God's enemies by Jesus the Lion. This is consistent with the Old Testament prophetic narrative concerning God's discipline of His people, which nonetheless ends in comfort, hope and restoration, and judgment of His enemies, both of which culminate on the Day of the Lord.

48. Day 7: Millennium

✝

Shabbat Shalom!

FOLLOWING the Day of the Lord, the dawn of the Millennium brings about the earthly *Shalom* of God - the consummation or bringing together into perfect union Man and God as Jesus rules the world through Israel His lesser light, the coming of true peace to mankind, and the Sabbath rest for both Man and God - Man resting in God, and God resting from His work of Creation. In a sense, we are brought back to the blessed state of Creation at the original Sabbath in Genesis 2, with one major difference as we will see shortly.

Feast of Tabernacles

Previously, we saw that the Day of the Lord will bring together the joint fulfilment of the first two Fall Feasts of God - the Feast of Trumpets summoning us to meet the Lord in the air, and the Day of Atonement when Jesus will return to the Mount of Olives to rescue and restore a repentant Israel while judging the nations. The Millennium is the fulfilment of the last of the 7 Feasts of God - the Feast of Tabernacles - and revolves around worship at the Millennial Temple. The Prophet Ezekiel gives us a detailed description of this Temple in Ezekiel 40-42, while Zechariah tells us that *"the survivors from all the nations that have attacked Jerusalem will go up year after year to worship the King, the LORD Almighty, and to celebrate the Festival of Tabernacles"* (Zechariah 14:16).

The Millennium ultimately reflects God's desire to tabernacle or live among us. We read in Zechariah 2:10-11 and Ezekiel 48:35," *"Shout and be glad, Daughter Zion. For I am coming, and I will live among you," declares the LORD. "Many nations will be joined with the LORD in that day and will become My people. I will live among you ... And the name of the city* [Jerusalem] *from that time on will be: THE LORD IS THERE* [*Yahweh Shammah*]." Jerusalem or *Yerushalayim*, which means the "City of Peace" - and by extension, the world and mankind - can only find true peace (*Shalom*) in God's presence.

Israel fulfills its original purpose

*I the Lord will be their God, and **my servant David will be prince among them** ... They will live in the land I gave to my servant Jacob ... and **David my servant will be their prince forever** ... The prince himself is the only one who may sit inside the gateway to eat in the presence of the Lord ... **It will be the duty of the prince to provide the ... offerings ... at all the appointed festivals of Israel***
- Ezekiel 34:24, 37:25, 44:3, 45:17

The Millennium also brings to pass all the unfulfilled Old Testament promises concerning Israel and the Kingdom of David - in particular David's greatest desire, which was to minister in God's presence in His Holy Temple. Israel will fulfill its original purpose as God's lesser light to the nations during the Millennium, with David - who will be among the resurrected - serving as Israel's prince in the Millennial Temple as seen in the verses above.

The redeemed *vs* the survivors

I mentioned at the start that the world will in a sense be restored to its original blessed state but with one major difference. Here, the description of the Millennial Kingdom in Revelations 20 and other related passages throughout the Bible seems to suggest that the Kingdom will comprise 2 groups - the first group being those redeemed by God (i.e., those who are part of the blessed "*first resurrection*") and the second group comprising "*survivors from all the nations.*"

The redeemed - which include David, the Apostles and likely only those who are martyred throughout history and the faithful still alive at Christ's return - will be clothed in glorified bodies and rule with Christ over these survivors, who remain in their fallen nature and will still experience death. Although greatly blessed by God during this thousand-year period, we are nonetheless told that as soon as Satan is released, many among these survivors will be deceived into rebelling against God one final time, with devastating eternal consequences. With this, the sun of time and history will finally set over the Final Day of Creation as the books are opened for the Final Judgment.

As we come to the end of the Seven Days of Creation, we are given Biblical insight into the remaining 2,000 years of human history from the time of Christ until now, as our generation awaits Jesus' soon return to usher in the Millennium (see diagram on the next page).

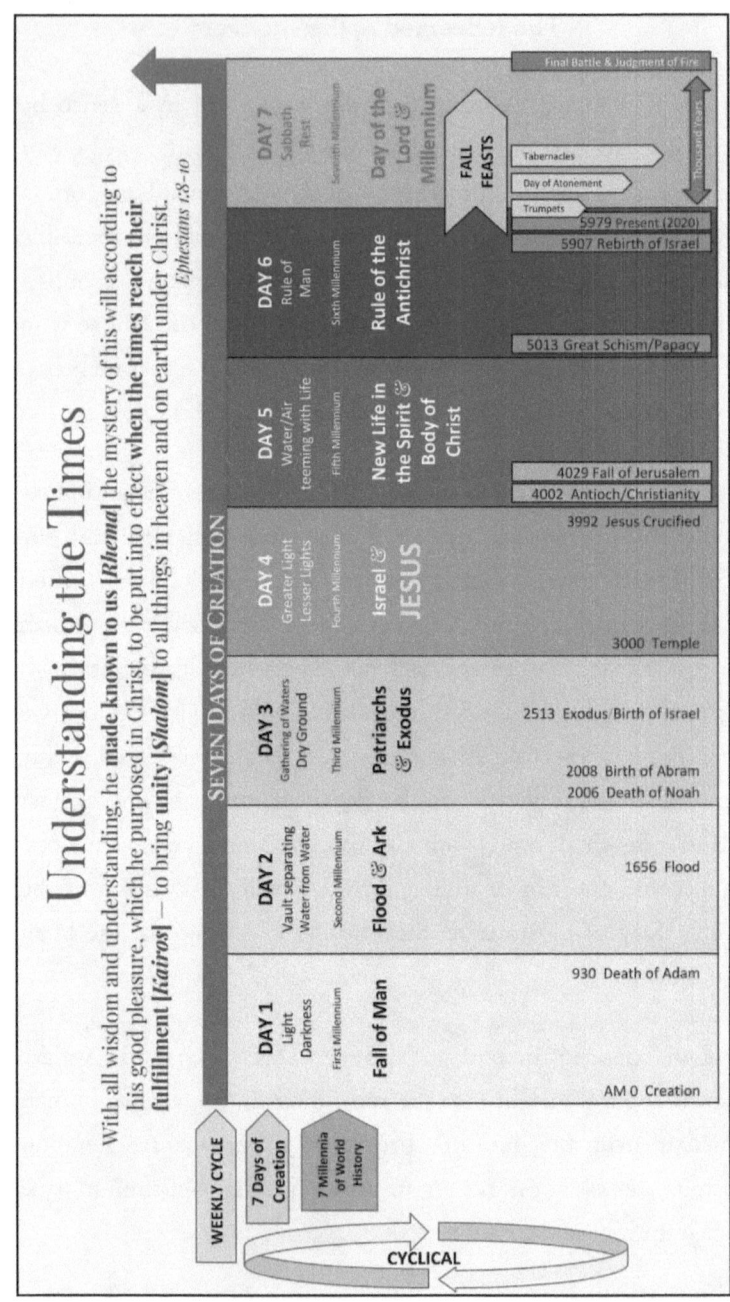

Here, **Day 5** foreshadows the **New Life in the Spirit and Body of Christ** available to all mankind through the giving of the Holy Spirit and birth of the Church as the Body of Christ. Now, although the Church was birthed at Pentecost, it was only with the emergence of the first Gentile Church in Antioch in AM 4002 - the beginning of the Fifth Millennium - that Christianity became a distinct faith. The Gentile Church would soon become God's means bringing His new life to the world for the next 2,000 years following the fall of Jerusalem and destruction of Israel in 70 AD.

However, wherever this new life in the Spirit of Christ has sprouted, the life-destroying spirit of the Antichrist has often quickly followed suit, manifesting itself in the kingdom and rule of man that tries to overthrow the Kingdom and Rule of God both in the world and in the Church.

Day 6 foreshadows this satanic spirit and coming **Rule of the Antichrist**. Beginning with the Great Schism and rise of the Papacy in AM 5013 - the start of the Sixth Millennium - Satan's attempt to rally the world against God will climax in the coming together of the State and Church in the end-time Roman-Babylonian Empire and Babylon the Prostitute.

With the rebirth of Israel in 1948 (AM 5907) 72 years ago, the stage is now set for the coming Tribulation as we in 2020 (AM 5979) approach the end of the Sixth Millennium in our generation.

This brings us to the events foreshadowed by **Day 7** - the final Day of Creation. Here, the Great Tribulation and with it God's discipline of His people and judgment of His enemies, climaxes with the return of Jesus the Lion of Judah, the King of Kings and Lord of Lords, on the **Day of the Lord**, as the armies of the world led by the Antichrist surround a desperate and repentant Israel who cries out for her *Messiah*.

In terms of the remaining Fall Feasts of the 7 Feasts of God, the Day of the Lord begins with the Feast of Trumpets - with the Final Trumpet announcing Christ's return and summoning the saints to meet the Lord in the air. This is followed by the Day of Atonement, the holiest and most solemn of all the Feasts, when Jesus returns and sets foot on the Mount of Olives to rescue and restore Israel, while judging the nations of the world. It is the one day when the sins committed by God's people the entire year are atoned for or covered - except that now, with Jesus' return, our sins are forgiven not for the year but for all eternity. However, for the wicked, they face the inevitable wrath of God's judgment once this Day - this Millennium - is over. The Fall Feasts end with the Feast of Tabernacles, symbolic of the Millennium itself when God will tabernacle or live among His people for a thousand years and mankind and all creation finally experience their earthly Sabbath rest.

The Millennium ends with a final battle and the final judgment of all mankind.

49. At Any Moment? Yes ... and No
✝

*For seven days present food offerings to the LORD, and on the **eighth day** hold a **sacred assembly** and present a food offering to the LORD. It is the **closing special assembly**; do no regular work*
- Leviticus 23:36

IN our overview of the 7 Days of Creation, we had briefly mentioned an "Eighth Day" Sabbath that Jews celebrate after the end of the 7-day Feast of Tabernacles prophetic of Christ's Millennial rule. According to Jewish tradition, after the Feast of Tabernacles, God invites His people to stay on for another day or Sabbath for a more intimate celebration.

The "Eighth Day" Sabbath marks the end of Creation and Time as we pass from this life into eternity. Here, the special Sabbath and closing assembly that is held is a picture of our eternal rest and communion with God as the Heavens, Earth and Time itself give way to the New Heaven and Earth and a New Jerusalem in eternity, spoken of in the final 2 chapters of Revelations.

Eternal rest and communion

If we recall, the spiritual realm is timeless and eternal. God gave us Time when He created the physical realm of the Heavens and the Earth. Now, as we return to eternity, what we know on earth as the beginning and end are one again in God, who is the "*Alpha and the Omega, the First and the Last, the Beginning and the End*" (Revelations 22:13). In Him, everything is now made complete, perfect and at rest (*Shalom*). God invites us to stay on for another day or Sabbath - which is none other than eternity itself - to have intimate communion and fellowship with Him forever.

Fullness of God's presence
- Every moment is *Rhema* and *Kairos*

The *Simchat Torah* or Rejoicing of the Torah, the first 5 books of the Bible, is also celebrated by Jews on this day to mark the end of the Torah public reading cycle. It is a picture of how the speaking out of God's Word at set times - in other words, God's cycle of *Rhema* and *Kairos* - will eventually end. From this point on, we will forever be in God's presence and every moment - if we can even speak of moments in eternity - is *Rhema* and *Kairos*.

Realising how close we are to the edge of time and how we can fall into the eternity of God's presence at any moment is what we want to look at next as we reflect on the imminence of the Second Coming of Christ - the often misunderstood idea that Christ may return at any moment and hence we cannot know when He is coming.

REFLECTIONS - On Imminence

Some of us, especially if we believe in a sudden rapture and return of Christ, may object that since we already know when Christ will return based on the 7 Days of Creation, His coming is no longer imminent - no longer something that can happen at any moment. Let me try to address this in terms of how the physical and the spiritual, time and eternity, *Rhema* and *Kairos* intersect in our lives.

Imminence in death - Christ's coming can be said to be imminent because we will meet the Lord the instant we die and we do not know when that will happen. Even on our deathbed, God can miraculously heal us or for that matter, He can even choose to resurrect us after we are dead! But the moment we truly die, we are taken out of *Chronos* time and instantly transported into God's presence - for those who are part of the First Resurrection, they will "time-jump" to that *Kairos* moment where they will meet the Lord in the air prior to the Millennium; for the rest of us, we will be taken out of Creation and Time completely to stand before God's Throne at the Final Judgment.

Imminence in ignorance and unbelief - We already learnt how, on this Sixth Day that we are living in now, the spirit of this age is not the Holy Spirit of Truth but the lying spirit of the Antichrist. There is so much deception around us and in the Church that many are unable to recognise - or choose not to believe - the signs of Christ's coming. It was the same with the Jews in Jesus' day - they could not recognise the *Messiah* even when He was standing right before their eyes. Yes, Christ will indeed come suddenly, unexpectedly, to those who are spiritually blind.

Today - The Eighth Day *Kairos*

*God again set a certain day [Kairos], calling it "****Today****"… "Today, if you hear His voice [Rhema], do not harden your hearts"* - Hebrews 4:7

This brings us to the verse above.

We spoke about God's *Rhema* and *Kairos* for His people so that we understand the times and know what we should do. What God wants to say to us can be discerned from the Bible when seen through the perspective of the 7 Days of Creation.

But there is also an Eighth Day *Kairos*, that split-second instant separating us from God's very presence in eternity, which is called "Today." And His *Rhema* for us in this *Kairos* Now is, "*Today, if you hear His voice [Rhema], do not harden your hearts.*"

The choice is ours to make … TODAY. For tomorrow may be too late.

Jesus said, "*Look, I am coming soon! My reward is with Me, and I will give to each person according to what they have done*" (Revelations 22:12, 20).

Are we ready? Have we done what we need to do to be confidently expectant of Jesus' soon return? We may be called to meet Him anytime, but perhaps even more worrying, we may not be called to meet Him yet - and in the meantime, we need to trim our lamps and make sure our oil is filled so that when Jesus finally shows up, we are not left in the dark and blind to His presence (Matthew 25:1-13).

50. Back to the *Kairos* Now
†

AS we conclude, I want to leave you with these 3 key messages:

ONE, we are fast approaching the end - We are in the twilight of the Sixth Day of Creation before the Seventh Day arrives at sunset, the end of the summer harvest before the Fall Feasts begin, the 70th Jubilee from the time Israel possessed the Promised Land and 40th Jubilee from the time of Jesus' first coming and birth of the Church, and the final generation that will witness His return.

TWO, we will be tested in unprecedented ways - Israel and the Church share a common prophetic destiny according to God's eternal will. Israel's rejection of Jesus at His first coming was part of the mystery of God's will opening the way for the salvation of the Gentile nations through the Body of Christ.

However, once the fullness of the Gentiles has come in, the keys of the Kingdom will be handed back to the Jews as the Church falls into deception and apostasy and this Apostate Church ultimately rejects Christ in favour of the Antichrist. We who are the true Gentile children of God will join in the sufferings of our Jewish brethren as God refines both them and us as one Body in Him in preparation for His coming.

THREE, we need to equip ourselves and others in the Body of Christ - In view of the coming flood and fire of apostasy and persecution, we need to uphold one another within our own fellowship groups and beyond to (1) keep the Faith, (2) persevere in Hope, and (3) Love the Body. We can only stand (and withstand) individually when we stand together with fellow saints of God, being one in Spirit as we look past our local church, denomination and the Church as a whole to embrace our Jewish brothers and sisters in ushering in God's Kingdom.

Issachar B7D Fellowship

from Issachar, men who understood the times and knew what Israel should do - 1 Chronicles 12:32

We spoke earlier of how, when David was rallying for support from the people to bring Israel under his rule following the death of King Saul, the men of the tribe of Issachar acted decisively to join him because they understood the times - meaning, God's will for the nation then - and knew what Israel should do. They looked past the interests of their own tribe to join together with the other tribes of Israel to usher in God's Kingdom rule through David.

In this *Kairos* Now, we believe that God is again speaking and releasing a similar message to His people.

We, like the men of Issachar, need to hear, understand and act decisively in light of God's *Rhema* and will to repair, rebuild and rescue His people and to release His prophetic word for this *Kairos* moment. We need to look past the interests of our own narrow "tribes" as it were to stand together with other like-minded saints and especially our Jewish brothers and sisters in Christ to rally behind and usher in the Kingdom of the Son of David, Jesus Christ.

We do this "*not by might nor by power*" (Zechariah 4:6) as the world does, but by His Word, Spirit and People that enables us to be overcomers in Faith, Hope and Love. As you study God's *Logos* together in your own fellowship groups in whichever local church or denomination you belong to, may His *Rhema* and Spirit transform you into such future and Christ-ready fellowships in His *Kairos*.

Amen!

www.ingramcontent.com/pod-product-compliance
Lightning Source LLC
LaVergne TN
LVHW041810060526
838201LV00046B/1201